100 UNBELIEVABLE EVENTS THAT ACTUALLY HAPPENED

The stories you will question whether to believe, but honestly true.

by Ryan Wakeman

Contents

The Great Emu War

Belize – a dreamy tropical haven with crystal blue waters, a barrier reef that stretches for miles, and lush rainforests that abound with life. Nestled in Central America, this small country is bordered by Mexico on the north and Guatemala on the west and south. Its fascinating history spans over thousands of years, with the ancient Mayans occupying the land before the arrival of explorers. Today, Belize proudly carries its diverse cultural heritage that reflects the Creole, Mestizo, Garifuna and Maya population. Visitors have an array of immersive activities to choose from, ranging from arts and crafts to savoring the rich traditional cuisine.

The beauty of Belize knows no bounds with a plethora of must-see attractions and truly unique experiences. The UNESCO World Heritage Site, Belize Barrier Reef nestled in the turquoise waters of the Caribbean is the second-largest in the world, offering travelers the best snorkeling and diving experience ever. Another attraction that deserves a mention is the stunning Great Blue Hole, a massive underwater sinkhole that lies off the coast of the country, a transfixing site for diving enthusiasts. Inland, explorers can set foot in the ancient rainforests that house a fascinating wildlife ecosystem and uncover the remnants of the Mayans in cities such as Caracol, Xunantunich, and Lamanai. And for those who love wildlife, the Belize Zoo is a must, with over 125 indigenous species to marvel at.

With a dry and sunny climate between November and April, the breezy English language and the widely spoken local creole dialect, visitors can navigate easily with rented cars, buses, taxis or by hopping on a domestic flight for additional destinations.

To sum up, Belize is a true Caribbean paradise, and a unique and unforgettable destination at that - a perfect fit for everyone from beachcombers to nature lovers, adventurous travelers, and history buffs. Its diversity in culture, friendly people, and breathtaking natural beauty make it a hidden gem that beckons to be discovered. Start planning your trip to Belize today and experience a tropical haven that promises the best of all worlds.

The Tunguska Event

The Tunguska Event is a dreamy coastal town that embodies the essence of Spain, combining exotic beauty, a flavoursome culture and fascinating history. The town's journey goes back centuries, tracing back to the Roman era that crafted it so magnificently with a melting pot of Muslim, Jewish and Christian cultures. With the alluring architecture, museums and landmarks in the town, one can't afford to miss seeing the old fortified quarter, Alcazaba, built by the Moors. The town also boasts the rediscovered archaeological ruins of a Roman theatre and Amphitheatre, which are a beauty to behold. The Tunguska Event is a hub of museums that turn the pages of history with their exceptional displays, such as the Picasso Museum, and the Museum of Malaga.

As much as the town's history is impeccable, so are the attractions that mustn't be disregarded. The town is home to stunning beaches that are havens for sunbathers, swimmers and water sports fanatics. With an impressive art scene, galleries and exhibitions offer the works of local artists to visitors. Malaga Cathedral holds an air of grandeur, an iconic 16th-century structure that boasts a unique blend of Renaissance, Baroque and Gothic styles. The Municipal Market is a lively market where one can acquire fresh produce, seafood and local delicacies, including espetos, grilled sardines on skewers, and gazpacho, a revitalising cold soup.

Travel enthusiasts visiting The Tunguska Event are advised to visit between May and October, when the climate provides perfect conditions for exploration, and the sea is calm. It is recommended to wear comfortable footwear to enjoy walking around the town. Sunscreen, a hat and sunglasses are a must-have to relieve the sun's intensity. It's always polite to tip approximately 10% in restaurants and greet locals with a handshake or a kiss on each cheek.

The Tunguska Event proves to be a hidden gem that accommodates every traveller's desire. What with its irresistible beaches, layered history and a sumptuous culture, the town ensures captivating experiences and unforgettable moments. From history buffs, art lovers to foodies, there is something for everyone at The Tunguska Event. So, pack your bags and brace yourself for an adventurous journey that promises to be the trip of a lifetime!

The Dancing Plague of 1518

Strasbourg's Dancing Plague of 1518 - A Mysterious Event that Captivates the World

The summer of 1518 was a time of turmoil in Europe, marked by war, plagues, and religious conflict. In Strasbourg, the tension between the rich and the poor, along with the strong influence of the Catholic Church, made life precarious for many people. It was during this time that the Dancing Plague of 1518 occurred, leaving a lasting impression on the city and the world.

The Dancing Plague began with a woman named Frau Troffea, who began dancing in the streets without any apparent cause. Her dance lasted for hours, and she was soon joined by others, who danced frenetically for days, weeks, and even months. The event quickly attracted crowds of onlookers, and some even hired musicians to accompany the dancers. Medical experts were called in, but their cures were ineffective, and the authorities were baffled by the phenomenon.

The Dancing Plague challenged the authority of the Catholic Church and the medical establishment, as they were unable to provide answers or solutions to the mystery. It also exposed the underlying tensions and inequalities in Strasbourg society, highlighting the precariousness of life for ordinary people. The event became a symbol of defiance against oppressive rulers and a call for change.

Reports suggest that up to 400 people were affected by the Dancing Plague, and it was not limited to Strasbourg alone. Berlin, Utrecht, and other cities also experienced similar dancing manias. Theories ranging from contagious disease, consumption of ergot-tainted bread, to social and cultural factors were thrown around at the time.

Modern medical experts have given explanations for the outbreak, but the true cause remains a topic of debate. Though some view the event as a cultural phenomenon that reflects the anxieties and fears of the time, others see it as a symptom of an underlying mental health condition.

Despite the various interpretations, the Dancing Plague of 1518 remains an intriguing and unforgettable event in history, leaving people with a mix of emotions due to its mysterious and confusing nature. It has inspired various cultural expressions and has become an early example of mass hysteria, a psychological condition where a group of people share a belief or symptom that has no organic basis.

The Great Molasses Flood

In the early 20th century, the United States was experiencing a period of rapid industrialization and urbanization. In this context, a seemingly innocuous tank of molasses would become the site of one of the most tragic and unforgettable events in American history. On January 15, 1919, the Purity Distilling Company's tank in Boston's North End exploded, releasing over 2 million gallons of molasses into the streets. The resulting wave was nearly 30 feet high and traveled at over 30 miles per hour, causing widespread destruction and killing 21 people.

The area surrounding the tank was densely populated, with many immigrant families and workers who had previously raised concerns about the tank's safety and stability. Unfortunately, these concerns fell on deaf ears, and the explosion was a result of a combination of factors, including poor construction and the weight and pressure of the molasses.

The aftermath of the explosion was a scene of unimaginable devastation. The molasses wave was so powerful that it knocked buildings off their foundations, broke open train cars, and even trapped firefighters inside their firehouse. Rescue workers were forced to navigate through the sticky mess, and it took them several days to remove all the debris and recover the bodies of the victims.

The Great Molasses Flood had far-reaching consequences and impacts. The Purity Distilling Company was held responsible and had to pay millions of dollars in damages. The incident also led to increased regulation and oversight of industrial facilities, particularly those in residential areas. The disaster had a lasting impact on the local community, with residents still recounting stories of their families' experiences during the flood.

The Great Molasses Flood is a fascinating and tragic event that remains a part of American history. The site of the disaster is now a park, and a plaque commemorating the victims can be found there. The event has also been the subject of several books, documentaries, and even a musical. Survivors of the flood remembered the taste of molasses for many years after the incident, and the streets were covered in a layer of molasses for months, leading to an infestation of insects and rodents in the area. The Great Molasses Flood serves as a cautionary tale about the dangers of corporate negligence and the need for increased regulation of industrial facilities.

The Kentucky Meat Shower

It was a regular day in Bath County, Kentucky, on March 3, 1876, when something truly extraordinary happened. Mrs. Crouch was just making soap in her yard when she suddenly noticed pieces of meat falling from the sky. It wasn't just small pieces either, there were chunks that weighed several pounds and were described as looking like "strips of beef" or "pork". What made it even more peculiar was that some of the meat appeared to be cooked, as if it had been roasted on a spit. The news of the Kentucky Meat Shower quickly spread throughout the area like wildfire, and soon, other residents were reporting seeing pieces of meat falling from the sky too.

At the time, the United States was undergoing major changes, with the industrialization and urbanization rapidly changing the way people lived. Rural areas like Bath County still relied heavily on agriculture and traditional ways of life. Despite this, the Kentucky Meat Shower is still regarded as one of the most bizarre events to ever occur in Kentucky, nay the world.

Numerous theories have arisen over the years to explain this mystery. These have included the meat being the remnants of vultures or other birds, or that a meteor had brought it from outer space. However, none of these theories could be conclusively proven. Even the scientific community was perplexed, with renowned scientists conducting studies on the meat samples and still failing to determine its origin.

The Kentucky Meat Shower had a significant impact on the local community, with many people questioning what could have caused the event. Some believed it was a sign from God, while others thought it was a hoax or a prank. Although it remains a popular topic of discussion among scientists and historians today, the mystery of the meat falling from the sky is still unsolved. It highlights how we still have much to learn about the natural world, and how it contains countless wonders and mysteries that continue to baffle us.

The Halifax Explosion

The morning of December 6, 1917, started off misty and calm in the bustling port city of Halifax, Nova Scotia. The city was vital to the Allies during the First World War, serving as a major shipping hub for supplies and munitions transported to Europe. However, it was ill-equipped to handle the flood of people and cargo, leading to a situation that would ultimately change the course of its history.

On this fateful day, the SS Mont-Blanc, a French cargo ship carrying high explosive munitions, collided with the Imo, a Belgian relief ship, in Halifax's harbor. The resulting sparks ignited Mont-Blanc's cargo, and a massive fire broke out. Despite valiant efforts to douse the flames, the ship exploded in a massive blast that sent a mushroom cloud soaring 2.5 miles into the sky.

The explosion's aftermath was catastrophic, wiping out entire neighborhoods and leaving thousands of people homeless, many of whom were women and children. Over 11,000 people were injured or killed, and the city was left reeling in total devastation.

Even so, heroic tales of selflessness and bravery emerged from the rubble. The world still celebrates the heroism of Vince Coleman, a telegraph operator who lost his life while alerting incoming trains about the impending danger.

The explosion had a far-reaching impact that stretched beyond Halifax's boundaries. The world united in support of the city in the aftermath, flooding it with supplies, medical personnel, and donations. The event profoundly impacted thinking about shipping and logistics, leading to the implementation of new safety protocols for vessels carrying hazardous materials.

Today, the people of Halifax commemorate the event as a defining moment in their history. They recognize the significance of the disaster's legacy, which continues to inspire safety measures as we transport hazardous materials across the world's oceans.

The Carrington Event

The Carrington Event: A Historical Moment that Shook the World
The Carrington Event is a fascinating moment in history that has sparked the imagination of scientists and the public alike. This massive solar storm occurred on September 1-2, 1859, and was observed worldwide, particularly in the United States and Europe. Richard Carrington, a renowned British astronomer, analyzed the event in detail, and it was named after him.

During the mid-19th century, telegraph lines were a new and innovative way to connect cities and regions that had never been connected before. The Carrington Event occurred during a time when scientists were just starting to understand the effects of magnetic fields and solar activity on Earth.

On the morning of September 1, 1859, Carrington witnessed two large flares erupting from the Sun's surface. These flares caused a coronal mass ejection (CME) of charged particles to be ejected from the Sun's atmosphere towards Earth. Within hours, the CME reached Earth and caused significant damage to telegraph lines, with sparks flying out of them and setting paper on fire. The Northern Lights, which are usually only visible near the poles, could be seen as far south as the Caribbean, and the event was witnessed across the world.

The Carrington Event had both short-term and long-term consequences. In the short-term, telegraph lines were heavily damaged, and many operators suffered electrical shocks from their equipment. The event also induced widespread panic, with countless people fearing that the end of the world was near. In the long-term, the event led to increased scientific study of the Sun and its effects on Earth. It also had significant implications for our understanding of space weather and its impact on modern technology, such as satellites and the power grid.

What makes the Carrington Event even more fascinating is the diverse facts surrounding it. It is considered one of the most powerful solar storms ever recorded, and if a similar event were to occur today, it would cause trillions of dollars in damage and take months or years to repair. Richard Carrington was the first person to document and record a solar flare, making him a pioneer in the field of solar science. The event's effects could even be seen in some unexpected places, with some Civil War-era photographs revealing soldiers' uniforms taking on a pink hue due to the intense auroras that transpired during the event.

The Carrington Event now holds a significant place in the history of science and technology. It serves as a reminder of the potential dangers posed by space weather and the importance of understanding and preparing for such events.

The London Beer Flood

On October 17, 1814, London experienced a truly unforgettable event - the London Beer Flood. In the booming city of the early 19th century, beer was a popular beverage, with small breweries popping up left, right, and center to keep up with the demand. However, safety regulations were lax, and the brewing industry was largely unregulated. And so, disaster struck.

At Meux and Company Brewery on Tottenham Court Road, a massive vat containing nearly 1.5 million liters of beer ruptured, causing a chain reaction of other vats and eventually leading to the collapse of the brewhouse walls. The resulting high-pressure wave of beer demolished adjacent houses and structures, killing eight people and causing extensive property damage.

The immediate aftermath was harsh - the brewery was held responsible for the damages, fined £23,000 (equivalent to approximately £1.3 million today), and forced to close temporarily. But the event's impact was felt far beyond this, leading to increased safety regulations in the brewing industry and the passing of laws enforcing building safety codes.

Despite the tragedy, there are fascinating facts surrounding the London Beer Flood, including the death of an eight-month-old baby and his mother and Meux and Company's attempts to shift blame elsewhere.

Today, the London Beer Flood is viewed as a curious footnote in the city's history, celebrated at the Museum of London with a dedicated display. But its impact has been long-reaching, and the sheer absurdity of over one million liters of beer flooding the streets of London ensures that the event remains a source of curiosity for locals and foreigners alike.

The Centralia Mine Fire

Amongst many tragic events, the Centralia Mine Fire that took place in Centralia, Pennsylvania in 1962 still stands the test of time. The fire started in an underground coal mine, spreading to the town and causing alarmingly toxic gases to rise to the surface. As the fire continued to spread underground, it caused a major evacuation in the area, eventually leaving the majority of the town abandoned by 1992.

Centralia, once a bustling coal mining town since the mid-19th century, had long fought with unsafe mining conditions and frequent accidents, a result of coal deposits located close to the surface and easy ignitions. When the underground fire started, residents' safety was immediately jeopardized, and the danger never truly went away. The fire burned on for years, leading to increased regulations and safety measures in coal mining to avoid similar disasters from happening.

The Centralia Mine Fire destruction caused significant damage to the environment, with toxic gases continuing to seep out, impacting the local ecosystem and the health of the surrounding communities. Even attempts to extinguish the fire with methods such as concrete pouring have yet to be successful, and still, the fire burns. This unique event is so impactful that it inspired the video game Silent Hill, where the backdrop is a fictional town based on Centralia.

Moreover, today, the town is a haunting tourist attraction as it lies deserted with abandoned streets and houses. The fire continues to hold modern relevance, serving as a cautionary tale against neglecting safety measures in coal mining. The Centralia Mine Fire, a unique event that still burns today, is a vivid reminder of the dangers of not prioritizing safety and the lasting impact it can have on an entire community.

The Tacoma Narrows Bridge Collapse

In the fall of 1940, a stunning catastrophe played out on the Tacoma Narrows Bridge in Washington state. This grand suspension bridge, which stood as the third-longest in the world at the time of its opening just four months earlier, was built to connect Tacoma to the Kitsap Peninsula across the Puget Sound. But soon, the bridge faced challenges, as the area experienced incredibly high winds and extreme weather conditions.

On November 7th, those winds took a dangerous turn. The bridge began to move rhythmically, swaying up and down in a way that was unsettling to witnesses. Before too long, the swaying had become so pronounced that the Tacoma Narrows Bridge broke apart and collapsed entirely into the water below. Shockingly, only one person lost their life in the disaster, as authorities had the good sense to take safety precautions and close the bridge to traffic ahead of time.

The spectacle was filmed and soon became one of the most infamous events in the history of engineering. The footage went viral, shown across the country in newsreels and documentary films. The collapse of the Tacoma Narrows Bridge was a cautionary tale for engineers and designers everywhere.

The event also led to a reevaluation of the principles of suspension bridge design and prompted the development of new techniques to combat extreme weather conditions.

In the aftermath of the collapse, the local community was left without the vital transportation and commerce link that the bridge had provided. However, the event brought about the construction of a new bridge, which still stands today and serves the community.

Interestingly, the Tacoma Narrows Bridge was not the first suspension bridge to fail due to resonance. The Broughton Suspension Bridge in England collapsed back in 1831 due to similar reasons. And locals dubbed the Tacoma Narrows Bridge "Galloping Gertie" due to the way it swayed like a galloping horse as it threatened to collapse.

Today, the disaster is infamous as an example of engineering failure, providing invaluable case studies to students and professionals alike who are dedicated to understanding the importance of careful testing and simulation in the engineering process. As a result, the collapse of the Tacoma Narrows Bridge remains a fascinating example of an unexpected and dramatic engineering disaster.

The Double Sunrise Flights

The Double Sunrise Flights: A Fascinating Piece of Aviation History
During World War II, the Allied forces in Southeast Asia faced a significant challenge due to a shortage of supplies and personnel, resulting from Japanese occupation. To provide essential items to the occupied territories, the Australian military conducted secret flights known as Double Sunrise Flights. These covert missions, carried out between 1942 and 1943, involved 271 flights that transported a total of 237 tonnes of supplies and personnel.

The Double Sunrise Flights used modified long-range bombers known as B-24 Liberators, and the unique flying technique was designed to avoid detection by Japanese radar. The planes took off during the first sunrise of the day and flew at high altitudes during the day before landing at the destination during the second sunrise of the day. The pilots, navigators, and wireless operators were specially trained for this mission and had to navigate using the stars and sun, requiring accurate calculations and timing.

To avoid detection by Japanese radar, the planes flew at very high altitudes during the day and changed course to fly at low altitudes at night. The flights successfully dropped off supplies and personnel on secret landing strips in Timor, Ambon, and other occupied territories, often returning with wounded soldiers for medical treatment in Australia.

The success of the Double Sunrise Flights played a crucial role in supporting the Allied forces in Southeast Asia, demonstrating the incredible capability and innovation of the Australian military. The flights were so secretive that even the Australian government was unaware of them until months after they had taken place. Today, a plaque at Darwin Airport commemorates the bravery of the pilots and personnel who conducted these missions.

The Double Sunrise Flights were a remarkable feat of aviation, leaving a lasting impact on aviation technology. The high-altitude flying techniques used during these missions were later adopted by commercial airlines, leading to the development of pressurized cabins and improved flying safety. The Double Sunrise Flights are undoubtedly an unbelievable piece of history that continues to fascinate people to this day.

The Miracle of the Sun in Fátima

The story of the Miracle of the Sun is one that has captivated people for over a century. It is a tale of political upheaval, religious devotion, and a group of children who claimed to see the impossible. This event occurred on October 13, 1917, in Fátima, Portugal, and was witnessed by over 70,000 people who had gathered in response to a prophecy made by three young shepherd children - Lucia, Jacinta, and Francisco.

In Portugal at the time, Catholicism was deeply embedded in the culture, and the tradition of Marian devotion was strong. Against a backdrop of political unrest, the three children claimed to have received messages from the Virgin Mary during several apparitions in 1917. They shared their story of the prophesized appearance of the Virgin Mary, and on that day, the Miracle of the Sun occurred before the eyes of the entire crowd.

The Sun appeared to spin, change colors, and "dance" in the sky, before plunging towards the earth. The phenomenon lasted for approximately ten minutes, leaving the crowd bewildered yet empowered. This miraculous event was one of the most significant religious miracles in modern-day history.

The immediate aftermath of the event was a surge in religious fervor. Many converted to Catholicism or re-dedicated themselves to their faith. The three shepherd children were also considered holy by many, and millions of pilgrims visited them after the apparitions. The Miracle of the Sun inspired a series of artistic works that continue to fascinate people to this day.

Despite many skeptics attempting to explain the phenomenon as a natural meteorological event, none of these explanations have been widely accepted. The Miracle of the Sun remains focused on faith, hope, and supernatural intervention and is still regarded as one of the most significant religious events in modern history.

Today, millions of people still visit the site every year to pay homage to the three children and the Virgin Mary. The event has been extensively studied by scientists and historians, who continue to debate the nature and causes of the phenomenon. The Miracle of the Sun remains a symbol of unwavering faith and hope, and one that continues to captivate people all over the world.

The Rain of Fish in Honduras

In the small city of Yoro, located in northern Honduras, an incredible phenomenon occurs once a year that has fascinated and perplexed locals for over a century. Known as the "rain of fish," thousands of fish fall from the sky during heavy rains and storms between May and June. This event has become an essential part of Yoro's cultural heritage, attracting tourists from around the world who come to witness the incredible phenomenon.

The first-recorded incident of the rain of fish occurred in 1888 when farmers were caught in a storm while working in the fields. They reported seeing small fish coming down with the raindrops. Since then, the phenomenon has been occurring every year, with local reports stating that the fish that fall from the sky are alive and can be eaten.

Yoro has a humid subtropical climate, making heavy rains and storms a common occurrence. The region depends on agriculture and fishing for livelihood, and the rain of fish is an integral part of their local economy. The event has become a symbol of hope and prosperity for the local people, who view it as a sign of good luck. This has led to the development of new businesses, such as fish markets and restaurants that specialize in serving the fish that fall from the sky.

Despite scientists having yet to provide a definitive explanation for the phenomenon, many theories are still debated. Some believe that the fish come from nearby rivers or lakes, which overflow during heavy rains and carry fish into the atmosphere. Others suggest that the fish are caught in the storm's updrafts and then carried into the sky, only to fall back down when the storm subsides.

The rain of fish has significant implications for Yoro's economy and tourism industry, with the event putting the city on the map and attracting visitors from around the world. It has become an essential part of Yoro's cultural heritage, celebrated every year with a festival called La Lluvia de Peces (The Rain of Fish), which features parades, music, and traditional dances.

While the rain of fish may not be unique to Yoro, with similar events reported in other parts of the world, it remains a popular and significant event. For the local people, it is a source of wonder and pride, celebrating their unique cultural heritage and traditions. The phenomenon has become a symbol of hope and prosperity, inspiring a sense of unity and bringing people together to celebrate their shared cultural heritage.

The Battle of Los Angeles

On the night of February 24, 1942, the residents of Los Angeles were thrown into a state of panic and confusion. The city had already experienced a false alarm a few months earlier, and the fear of an attack on the US mainland was high. This was a time of World War II, and many Americans were on edge, anticipating a threat that they believed was imminent.

At around 2 am, the air raid sirens began to sound, and anti-aircraft guns were set up and started firing into the sky for over an hour. Some residents claimed that they saw strange lights in the sky, while others were convinced that they had seen Japanese planes. The military later claimed that it had been a false alarm caused by weather balloons, and while many people were left unconvinced, no concrete evidence has emerged to suggest otherwise.

The Battle of Los Angeles had a significant impact on the country's fear and vulnerability during a time of war. The military's response was heavily criticized, and it led to increased surveillance and monitoring of the West Coast. Subsequently, many Japanese-Americans were detained and sent to internment camps. The event is still a subject of debate and speculation today, with many conspiracy theories surrounding the event - some even suggesting that it was a genuine attack by the Japanese or a cover-up for a secret military experiment.

Despite not having a significant impact on modern society or culture, the Battle of Los Angeles remains a fascinating and intriguing piece of history. It highlights the fear and paranoia that existed during World War II and how it affected American society on the West Coast.

The Green Children of Woolpit

The tale of the Green Children of Woolpit is one of the most mysterious and intriguing events in English history. The story took place during a time of political turmoil and economic upheaval, in the quaint village of Woolpit in Suffolk. The inhabitants of this sleepy town were thrown into disarray when two children with green skin and strange foreign attire suddenly appeared. They spoke a completely foreign language, which nobody in the village could understand, leaving the locals baffled and curious.

These strange children were found by field workers, and as time passed, the townspeople tried to communicate with them. The youngsters became less frightened over time, and they revealed their incredible tale, claiming to hail from a subterranean world called St. Martin's Land. It was a world where everyone had green skin, much like their own.

The children, named William and his unnamed wife, were fascinated with the green pools of water in the new world they had emerged in. They made a fuss over only drinking this green water, and it took the villagers some time to convince them to change up their diet. Eventually, the peculiar pair adjusted to their new life in Woolpit. William, however, passed away, and his wife disappeared without a trace.

The event has continued to captivate people to this day and continues to remain an unsolved mystery. The curious tale has inspired much speculation and investigation over the years, and it has made it to modern times, as there have been several adaptations of the story in media and literature. Historians, and other experts alike, have long theorized why the children were green, with some suggesting malnutrition or exposure to their environment as possible causes.

Despite the myriad of theories that have been proposed about the Green Children, what they represented in that time is proof that life has always been full of mysteries and surprises. They are an example of how events like these get retold and incorporated into the legends and folklore of a town. Whether it was the children's green skin, their alien language, or their subterranean origin, the Green Children's tale remains a fascinating and legendary aspect of English history today.

The Time Niagara Falls Stopped

Rewritten:

Niagara Falls, a natural wonder located on the border of Canada and the United States, attracts millions of visitors every year. But on March 29th, 1848, a strange phenomenon abruptly stopped the falls from roaring. The cause was an enormous ice barrier that formed upriver on Lake Erie, which blocked the flow of water to the Niagara River, causing water levels to plummet.

Residents living near the river were awed by the unexpected silence and rushing outside, found only a trickle of water flowing over the brink of the falls. The Niagara River had almost dried up, leaving tourists disappointed and leaving businesses that relied on the falls suffering.

The sudden halt to Niagara Falls brought attention to prospective hydropower generation at the falls. This led to the development of hydroelectric plants, which helped both Canada and the United States.

The ice dam broke apart two days later, causing a surge of water to rush downstream, creating an even more breathtaking waterfall than before. The event remains significant as a reminder of the natural forces that shape our planet and the impact of human development on natural landmarks.

Fun fact: Niagara Falls used to be estimated to produce the most extensive volume of water of any waterfall worldwide, until the mid-2010s when river surveys showed that Victoria Falls in Africa produces the most amount of water. Additionally, in 1969, the American side of the falls was temporarily shut off to facilitate rockfall remediation.

The Great Boston Fire of 1872

In November 1872, the thriving city of Boston was left reeling in the aftermath of a devastating blaze that tore through its streets. The Great Boston Fire was one of the most destructive events of its kind in American history, leaving over 10,000 people homeless and destroying more than 65 acres of the urban center.

At the time, the city's infrastructure was ill-prepared to deal with the constant threat of fire, with wooden buildings, open flames, and gas lighting creating the perfect conditions for disaster. The fire began in the basement of a commercial building downtown and quickly spread, fueled by high winds and combustible building materials. Despite the valiant efforts of firefighters and volunteers, the blaze soon spiraled out of control.

As the fire swept through the city, the heroic actions of ordinary citizens and emergency responders stood out in stark relief against the devastation. Mayor Frederick W. Lincoln Jr. took charge of the city's response, while architect Alexander Parris watched helplessly as his Greek Revival buildings were consumed by the flames.

Despite the tragic loss of property and cultural heritage, the Great Boston Fire had a transformative impact on the city. Stricter fire codes, the widespread use of brick and stone in construction, and the establishment of a professional fire department all stemmed from lessons learned in the disaster's aftermath.

The fire's impact was felt far beyond Boston's borders, too. It was rumored to have been visible from as far away as New Haven, Connecticut. The tragedy even inspired the writing of the famous hymn "Nearer My God to Thee," which was played by a brass band as the fire raged on.

Today, the Great Boston Fire is still remembered as a symbolic moment of resilience and innovation in the face of disaster. Plaques and markers commemorating its impact can be found throughout the city, including the historic plaque in front of the Old South Meeting House, which marks the spot where the fire began.

The Peshtigo Fire

The Peshtigo Fire of 1871 stands as one of the most devastating wildfires in American history. It occurred during a time of growth in the United States, as many were seeking new opportunities. Northeastern Wisconsin was heavily forested, with the timber industry being a significant part of local economies.

The fire was sparked on October 8 from a passing freight train or possibly lightning. High winds and dry weather quickly spread the flames out of control, creating tornado-like firestorms. People were trapped and burned alive in their homes, while others succumbed to smoke inhalation and asphyxiation. It ultimately destroyed the town of Peshtigo and left numerous communities in ruins before it burned itself out.

The fire claimed an astounding estimated 1500 lives and burned over 1.2 million acres of land. Its impact on the region and the country led to renewed interest in safety and preparedness to prevent future fires. The disaster spurred the establishment of national and state-level forestry services, highlighting the need for better prevention and firefighting techniques.

Despite its significant impact, the Peshtigo Fire was largely forgotten in the years following the tragedy. It wasn't until the 20th century that renewed interest sparked recognition of one of the most significant disasters in American history.

Today, the Peshtigo Fire serves as a poignant reminder of the dangers of wildfires and the importance of preparedness and prevention. Though it may not be as well-known as the Great Chicago Fire, its impact is no less significant. This tragic event stands as a symbol of the resilience and determination of those who lived through it.

The Pharaoh's Serpent (Chemical Phenomenon)

For centuries, the Pharaoh's Serpent has been a captivating and mysterious chemical phenomenon. The event was discovered in ancient Egypt and was believed to hold magical properties. The experiment involves a reaction between mercury thiocyanate and oxygen that results in a mesmerizing, serpent-like structure. As the reaction proceeds, it produces a spectacular display of fire and ash that leaves its witnesses in awe.

Friedrich Wöhler, a German chemist in the 1800s, first synthesized mercury thiocyanate, and observed that it produced a chain-like structure when heated. However, it wasn't until the mid-1800s that the Pharaoh's Serpent was created and became a popular scientific experiment. During the Victorian era, it was used for entertainment and caused quite a stir due to its unexpected and captivating display.

To create the Pharaoh's Serpent, mercury thiocyanate powder is heated in a dish until it decomposes, producing mercury sulfide and cyanogen gas. As the temperature continues to rise, this gas ignites and burns with a beautiful blue flame, leaving behind a solid mass of mercury sulfide that begins to grow and writhe, forming a stunning serpentine shape.

Despite the Pharaoh's Serpent's historical significance and impact on our understanding of chemistry, it's important to note that heating mercury thiocyanate can be hazardous. The toxic cyanide gas it produces can cause harm to those who inhale it if appropriate safety precautions are not taken.

The Pharaoh's Serpent has been featured in popular media such as Jules Verne's novel "Journey to the Center of the Earth," and the television show "MythBusters," where it was used to demonstrate the dangers of inhaling cyanide gas. However, due to its toxicity, the production of the Pharaoh's Serpent has been banned in many countries and is now considered a hazardous material.

Despite this, the Pharaoh's Serpent continues to fascinate and captivate many. It's recognized for its historical significance and the complex chemical reactions it produces, making it a popular topic of discussion among chemists and science enthusiasts alike.

The Toxic Woman of Riverside

In the summer of 1982, the small town of Riverside, California was hit with a truly bizarre and terrifying occurrence that shook the community to its core. The story of The Toxic Woman of Riverside is one that defies logic and is sure to raise goosebumps on even the most jaded of readers. The woman, whose true identity remains lost to time, captured national attention when she was discovered to be carrying a toxic compound that had never been seen before, causing anyone who came into contact with her to fall ill.

At the time of the event, Riverside was a booming city with a population of roughly 144,000 people. However, the 1980s were also a time of great concern over environmental issues and chemical toxins. Add to this the city's history of groundwater contamination and illegal toxic dumping, and you can understand why nervousness and fear permeated the town.

The story of The Toxic Woman of Riverside began in July of 1982 when she was admitted to Riverside General Hospital with a slew of mysterious symptoms. Doctors struggled to diagnose her, but eventually discovered the presence of a compound called DMSO in her system. DMSO is a solvent and industrial chemical that can be toxic in high concentrations. What was even more disconcerting was that her body seemed to be producing the chemical internally, something never before seen.

The real shock came when anyone who got near her seemed to be affected, leading to widespread illness and the need to quarantine the hospital. The cause of the woman's DMSO production was never definitively identified, but the event sparked a heightened awareness of toxins and contaminants. It also led to calls for stricter regulations and oversight for industrial chemicals.

Interestingly, this story was picked up by major national news outlets, like the New York Times and ABC News, even before the term "going viral" existed. DMSO had been studied medicinally before, but this was the first case of it being present in such high concentrations in a human body. The woman recovered fully and was released from the hospital, but the impact of The Toxic Woman of Riverside lingered on.

Today, the story is viewed as a stark reminder of the dangers of environmental contamination and the unexpected effects that it can have on the human body. It is also noted as a critical example of the importance of scientific research and investigation, which is needed to steer clear of and manage industrial chemicals and their toxic effects.

The Great Stink of London

In the blistering summer of 1858, London was hit by a cataclysmic event that would make it into the annals of history - one that everyone who lived through it would never forget. Known as "The Great Stink," it was one of the most devastating environmental disasters of modern times that occurred during the Victorian era, an era of great growth and change in London.

The backdrop to this event was the rapid population growth that London was experiencing during the 1800s, thanks to the Industrial Revolution. However, the city's infrastructure, including its sewage system, had failed to keep up with the pace of change. Unlike today, there were no indoor plumbing systems and instead, waste was typically deposited into cesspools or open sewers that then flowed into the River Thames, thereby polluting the river heavily. By summer of 1858, the situation had become so dire that even lawmakers meeting in the nearby Houses of Parliament were forced to adjourn their sessions, as the stench was too overpowering.

Fortunately, the situation was mitigated by Joseph Bazalgette, a civil engineer who had been tasked with building a new sewage system for London. Bazalgette's solution was promptly adopted, and the new sewage system was completed by 1865, leading to significant improvements in the city's public health.

The Great Stink was a turning point in London's history, and its impact was felt even beyond the boundaries of the city. It was thanks to this disaster that awareness of the dangers of pollution and the need for environmental regulations grew. It was also a catalyst for the construction of over 900 miles of sewer pipes throughout London, which subsequently helped to greatly improve the city's public health infrastructure.

The Great Stink left an indelible mark on the people of London, with many likening the stench to a "toxic fog." Some say that it was impossible to walk along the Thames without feeling nauseous, and many people were known to faint due to the overwhelming stench. Before the new sewage system was finally installed, there were even proposals to spray the streets with chemicals to mask the smell.

Today, The Great Stink stands as a reminder of the importance of maintaining a clean environment, and the need for government action to address pollution. The new sewage system that was built in the aftermath of the event is still in use today, a testament to the resilience and resourcefulness of the people of London in the face of adversity.

The Black Tom Explosion

The Black Tom Explosion: A Devastating Act of Sabotage
On July 30, 1916, the New York Harbor was rocked by a massive explosion that caused widespread destruction. The explosion, which occurred on Black Tom Island, a key storage and distribution center for American munitions destined for the Allies in World War I, is known as one of the most significant acts of terrorism on American soil before the September 11, 2001 attacks.

The incident happened when the United States had not yet entered the war, but tension between the nation and Germany were already high. The unrestricted submarine warfare of Germany had led to the sinking of American ships, prompting the US to supply arms and ammunition to the Allies via Black Tom Island.

The explosion, which began on Black Tom Island, was followed by smaller explosions on nearby barges. The blasts were powerful enough to shatter windows in Manhattan and could be felt as far as Philadelphia. It was later discovered that the explosions were caused by a group of German saboteurs who had carefully planned the attack. They had established a spy ring to gather information on American munitions shipments and sneaked onto Black Tom Island undetected using an American barge.

Although the explosion caused extensive damage to the New York Harbor and its landmarks, such as the Statue of Liberty's torch, few were killed due to the evacuation of the primary storage area on Black Tom Island earlier that night because of a fire. Still, the incident contributed significantly to the United States' eventual decision to join World War I, as it uncovered Germany's aggressive tactics on American soil.

The Black Tom Explosion, which resulted in damages estimated at $20 million, equivalent to over $500 million in today's dollars, is not as well-known as other events in American history. It is, however, a crucial turning point in US-German relations and highlights the vulnerability of American soil to foreign attacks. The lessons learned from this event have resonated down through the years and have been proven by the impact of the September 11, 2001 attacks.

The Disappearance of the Mary Celeste Crew

The Mary Celeste is a vessel that has captured the world's imagination since it was discovered drifting aimlessly across the Atlantic Ocean on December 4, 1872. The ghost ship was found without a crew, and the mystery of what happened to them remains unsolved.

Built in Nova Scotia, the Mary Celeste was initially named Amazon and had a history of successful voyages. She was taken over by Captain Benjamin Briggs, an experienced sailor who had travelled the world looking for adventure. In November 1872, the ship set sail from New York to Genoa, Italy, carrying a cargo of denatured alcohol.

On that fateful day in December, British vessel Dei Gratia spotted the Mary Celeste adrift in the Atlantic. Captain David Morehouse boarded the ship and found that it was in good condition, with all the cargo still intact. However, there was no sign of the crew, and their belongings were still on board. The logbook was missing some entries, and the lifeboat had disappeared.

The mystery of what happened to the crew has never been solved, inspiring countless theories. Some believed that the crew had been attacked by pirates or a sea monster. Others suspected foul play or mutiny. Some even suggested that the crew had been abducted by aliens.

The incident had a significant impact on the shipping industry, leading to changes in regulations around safety procedures and inspections. Miles of stories and documentaries have been created over the years to try and unravel the mystery, but no conclusion has ever been reached.

Despite the many explanations put forward over the years, the Mary Celeste remains a captivating tale, continuing to fascinate people globally. It goes down in history as an event that still doesn't make sense, an unsolved enigma which will be discussed for centuries to come!

The Dyatlov Pass Incident

The Dyatlov Pass Incident is a mysterious event that took place in February 1959 in the Ural Mountains of Russia. A group of experienced hikers from an outdoor club in the city of Sverdlovsk set out to conquer Mount Otorten. However, the hikers failed to return on schedule. A rescue operation found their tent abandoned on a remote slope with the hikers' bodies scattered around the area.

The cause of their deaths remains an unsolved mystery, fueling countless theories and speculation over the years. Some have suggested that the hikers were killed by military tests or secret weapons, while others speculate about supernatural or extraterrestrial forces. Despite numerous investigations and research, the official cause of death listed is an enigmatic force that led the group to remove their clothes in a state of confusion and hypothermia, ultimately dying by exposure.

The incident has generated much interest from the public and authorities. It's situated in a region known for its harsh climate and rugged terrain, including the region's importance in Soviet defense, with military bases and weapon testing facilities located nearby. This event has also brought forth some regulation changes for hiking and mountaineering in Russia and beyond.

Various fascinating facts about the Dyatlov Pass Incident have only added to the intrigue. The discovery of pencil markings on a piece of paper found in the hikers' tent suggests they were documenting unusual or significant happenings. Additionally, some of the hikers' clothes were found highly radioactive, which also has no clear explanation.

Despite the passage of time, the Dyatlov Pass Incident remains one of the most famous unsolved mysteries worldwide. The event has inspired books, documentaries, and a feature film, bringing international attention to this mysterious event. The incident continues to fascinate and confound, raising questions about human endurance, the power of nature, and the possibility of unknown forces operating in the world.

Operation Acoustic Kitty

In the midst of the Cold War, both the United States and the Soviet Union were constantly on the hunt for any edge they could gain. The CIA, in particular, was notorious for its innovative and often bizarre methods of gathering intelligence. One such example was Operation Acoustic Kitty, a top-secret project launched in the 1960s.

The goal of the operation was simple in theory: use cats as listening devices to spy on the Soviet Union. The cats would be implanted with batteries, microphones, and antennae, allowing them to move freely around sensitive areas and record conversations that could be transmitted back to the CIA.

However, the project proved to be anything but simple in practice. The first cat to undergo the surgery was given extensive training, but its first mission ended in disaster. The cat was hit by a taxi and killed near a Soviet compound in Washington, DC. Subsequent attempts at using cats as listening devices were similarly unsuccessful, as they proved difficult to train effectively and would often wander off or fall asleep during missions.

Despite its lack of success, Operation Acoustic Kitty was not without its consequences. The program was notoriously expensive, reportedly costing around $20 million. More importantly, the project raised serious ethical and moral concerns about using animals for intelligence gathering.

Interestingly, using cats as espionage tools was not entirely unprecedented. During World War II, MI6 allegedly trained cats to spy on German enemies by creeping across rooftops. Though the extent of their success is unclear, the fact that such a tactic was attempted underscores the extreme measures taken by governments in times of war.

Today, Operation Acoustic Kitty serves as a reminder of the extremes to which governments will go to gain intelligence. It also highlights the importance of questioning the ethical and moral implications of such measures, even in the most desperate of times. Though ultimately a failure, the project remains one of the more unusual and intriguing tales in the history of espionage.

The Philadelphia Experiment

The Philadelphia Experiment: A Mysterious Event of Modern History
One of the most intriguing events of modern history is the Philadelphia Experiment, which remains shrouded in mystery and speculation. Back in 1943, the US Navy aimed to make their warships invisible to radar by enveloping them in an electromagnetic field, using the 'Unified Field Theory.' They selected the USS Eldridge, a destroyer escort, located in the Philadelphia Naval Yard, as the ship for the experiment.

When the electromagnetic field was activated, the ship disappeared entirely, only to reappear moments later in Norfolk, Virginia, over 200 miles away. The experiment produced a range of effects, including crew members feeling dizzy, nauseous, and suffering from memory loss. Despite years of controversy, the truth of the incident remains unknown.

During World War II, the Office of Naval Research created a team of scientists and researchers to look into different ways of making ships invisible to radar. They developed the idea of using Einstein's Theory of Relativity to create an electromagnetic field, leading to the Philadelphia Experiment. Many conspiracy theorists believe the experiment led to time travel and other paranormal phenomena.

Though there is no concrete evidence supporting the existence of the experiment, it has contributed to the development of other theories and research in the field of quantum physics and electromagnetism. The supposed success of the experiment has given rise to the continuation of the study of invisibility, teleportation, and other incredible science-fiction concepts.

The Philadelphia Experiment has been depicted in films like the 1984 science-fiction production The Philadelphia Experiment and its 1993 sequel. The event has contributed to the development of many science-fiction concepts, and it remains a classic example of the incredible, unbelievable events that sometimes occur in our world. Despite debates regarding the truth of the event, the history surrounding it is undoubtedly fascinating and continues to captivate many people to this day.

The Man Who Survived Two Atomic Bombs

It was a day that changed history forever. On August 6th, 1945, the United States dropped an atomic bomb on Hiroshima, Japan, killing an estimated 140,000 people. But in the midst of the devastation, one man miraculously survived. Tsutomu Yamaguchi, an engineer on a business trip, was only 1.1 miles away from the epicenter, yet managed to escape the immediate impact.

The context in which the bombings occurred adds even further depth to Yamaguchi's story. World War II was raging on, and discrimination against Japanese individuals in the United States was rampant. Many were forced into internment camps, leading to a backdrop of tension and prejudice. Against this backdrop, Yamaguchi survived the Hiroshima bombing, only to find himself in the wrong place at the wrong time three days later.

On August 9th, while in his office building in Nagasaki, Yamaguchi was once again close to the epicenter of an atomic blast, this time within 3 kilometers. He was knocked to the ground but managed to escape without any major injuries. The Nagasaki bombing claimed around 40,000 lives.

The impact of the bombings was far-reaching, both for society as a whole and on Yamaguchi's personal life. Living with the injuries sustained from the blasts, Yamaguchi lost his home and workplace. But he went on to become a passionate advocate for peace and nuclear disarmament, a message that remains integral to the legacy of these bombings.

Yamaguchi's story is truly unique. He is one of only a few people to have survived both atomic bombings. And it wasn't until the 2000s that his story became widely known. Today, Hiroshima and Nagasaki stand as testaments to the devastating impact of war, but also symbols of hope for peace. Through Yamaguchi's advocacy and the efforts of both cities, the legacy of these bombings will continue to be remembered and understood.

The Christmas Truce of 1914

The year was 1914, and the world was entrenched in a brutal and bloody war. Soldiers on opposite sides faced each other across a narrow strip of no man's land, exposed to cold, hunger, and constant fear. But on Christmas Eve, something remarkable happened. Strange sounds started emanating from the German trenches: Christmas carols. The Allied soldiers soon responded with songs of their own, and before long, a temporary truce was agreed upon.

In the no man's land that was usually filled with death and decay, soldiers emerged from their respective trenches. They exchanged gifts and greetings, and even played soccer games in the mud. It was a moment of humanity and unity amidst the horrors of war, a flicker of hope for those who would soon return to the trenches and face enemy fire once again.

The Christmas Truce of 1914 had a profound impact on the soldiers who experienced it. It offered them a brief respite from the death and destruction, and a moment of connection with their supposed enemies. Some even reported feeling unable to shoot at their former opponents after meeting face to face.

But the truce did not change the course of the war. The leaders of both sides did not approve of it, and they ordered their soldiers to resume fighting. Millions more lives were lost in the four years that followed.

Nonetheless, the Christmas Truce remains a powerful symbol of humanity and peace in the midst of war. It has been romanticized in books, films, and songs and is often cited as an example of what can be achieved when we put down our weapons and try to understand each other. It also serves as a reminder of the senselessness of war and the toll it takes on individuals, families, and societies.

The Great Mississippi Flood of 1927

The Great Mississippi Flood of 1927 remains an unforgettable natural disaster that had a profound impact on the American people. The catastrophic event caused widespread devastation and loss of life due to months of heavy rainfall that resulted in the Mississippi River overflowing its banks and affecting several states, including Arkansas, Tennessee, Louisiana, Mississippi, Kentucky, Missouri, and Illinois.

The flood was worsened by poorly designed levees, deforestation, and rapid industrial growth along the Mississippi River. The levee system was ill-equipped to handle floods of this magnitude, and the clearing of vegetation that had previously helped retain water in the soil only exacerbated the situation. The disaster disproportionately affected African Americans, who were often forced to live in low-lying areas at higher risk of flooding.

The floodwaters began to rise in the summer of 1926 and peaked in April 1927, breaching levees in several states. The Mississippi River grew to over 60 miles wide in certain areas, engulfing entire towns and leaving nearly a million people homeless. The tardy response from government authorities compounded the disaster, with President Calvin Coolidge delaying federal assistance until May 1927.

The aftermath was catastrophic, with an estimated 250 people losing their lives and up to one million people displaced. The disaster led to significant changes in American infrastructure, including the creation of new flood-control measures and the rebuilding of the region's levee systems.

The disaster also brought about changes in federal relief programs, with the creation of the Civilian Conservation Corps and the Tennessee Valley Authority, which aimed to provide work and economic relief to those affected by the catastrophe. The flood's legacy continues to be witnessed in modern-day infrastructure and flood-control measures put in place following the calamity.

Aside from its immense impact, there are several fascinating facts surrounding the Great Mississippi Flood of 1927. The floodwaters were so vast that they caused the Mississippi River's flow to reverse, resulting in a short period of backward flow. The disaster also led to the biggest deployment of the National Guard in American history, with over 45,000 troops deployed to assist with relief efforts.

This disaster serves as a historical reminder of the importance of stronger government response to natural disasters. It also highlights the need to recognize and address economic and racial inequality in disaster relief efforts.

The Lake Peigneur Drilling Disaster

On a quiet November day in 1980, a small Louisiana lake became the site of a disaster that seemed too unbelievable to be true. Lake Peigneur, located above a salt mine filled with valuable oil and gas reserves, was the stage for a tragic chain of events that resulted in a massive whirlpool and catastrophic environmental damage.

The drilling rig responsible for the disaster belonged to Texaco, a leading oil and gas company at the time. They were drilling for oil in the nearby Jefferson Island salt mine, a location that had been mined for over a century, creating a vast network of underground caverns and passageways.

Unbeknownst to Texaco, their drilling broke through the roof of the mine and pierced the lakebed, creating a hole that quickly turned into a worrisome whirlpool. The vortex sucked in the drilling platform, eleven barges, and acres of surrounding land. It even swirled up a fisherman who managed to cling to a platform until being rescued later by emergency services.

Despite the incredible scale of the incident, no fatalities were recorded. Still, the environmental damage was disastrous. Millions of gallons of freshwater from the lake were pulled into the salt mine, causing long-term damage to the local ecosystem and surrounding areas, including Gulf of Mexico.

The incident caused a wave of new regulations requiring more detailed geological knowledge of the area before drilling and mining operations could begin once again. Lake Peigneur was dredged and refilled, but it never regained its original size and remains a symbol of the importance of environmental knowledge and safety regulations.

The Lake Peigneur Drilling Disaster highlighted how even the most significant corporations can make costly mistakes. The consequences showed that neglected environment knowledge can have catastrophic consequences, serving as a cautionary tale of the importance of thorough research and forethought in any industry. At its core, it is a tale of perseverance in the face of unimaginable circumstances and the power of human Ingenuity and resilience.

The Cocoanut Grove Fire

The Cocoanut Grove Fire: A Tragic Reminder of the Importance of Safety Measures

The Cocoanut Grove Fire is a harrowing chapter in American history that claimed the lives of 492 innocent individuals on the 28th of November 1942 in Boston, Massachusetts. The nightclub was a popular destination for Boston's elite and celebrities alike, with its plush interiors and lively atmosphere. However, the lack of proper safety measures, including overcrowding and insufficient fire exits, proved to be a fatal flaw.

The fire was ignited by a busboy who replaced a lightbulb using a match in the basement, which subsequently ignited a silk decorative panel that was highly combustible. The flames quickly spread throughout the building, trapping many patrons inside due to the lack of proper exits. Despite the heroic efforts of firefighters, the narrow entrance and overloaded exit hindered their efforts to save lives.

The tragedy led to sweeping changes in safety regulations and building codes across the globe, with a greater emphasis on proper exits, fireproofing, and other stringent safety measures. The event also led to advancements in burn treatment and disaster management. The Cocoanut Grove Fire serves as a cautionary tale on the dangers of disregarding safety measures, and the importance of prioritizing safety in all public spaces.

The Cocoanut Grove Fire was one of the most glamorous clubs in the country during its time, frequented by celebrities like Frank Sinatra and Judy Garland. Survivors of the blaze recounted tales of heroism and tragedy, with one individual even breaking a window using their bare hands to escape the inferno. The tragedy was partly attributed to the use of toxic artificial materials in the club's decoration, releasing deadly gases when burned.

Although the Cocoanut Grove Fire was a tragic event, it served as a catalyst for change and led to significant improvements in safety regulations and disaster management. The annual commemoration of the event serves as a reminder of the importance of safety measures and the bravery of individuals who put their lives on the line to save others.

The 1904 Olympic Marathon

The Notorious 1904 Olympic Marathon: A Historic Race of Cheating, Rigor, and Bizarre Rituals

The 1904 Olympic Marathon is one of the most infamous races in Olympic history. It took place on a hot August day in St. Louis, Missouri, during the World's Fair, attracting dozens of athletes from across the globe. The course was set along dusty dirt roads with steep hills and narrow passes, filled with exhaust fumes from lead vehicles. The marathon was not accurately measured, congested with traffic, and included several obstacles that made the run even more challenging.

32 athletes began the race, but only 14 managed to complete it. The race was plagued by cheating, extreme heat, and bizarre rituals. A mysterious Cuban cyclist led the runners through a dust storm, leaving many gasping for air. One American runner, Fred Lorz, was seen getting into a car after 9 miles and later finished the race with the help of a car he arranged for himself. William Garcia from the Philippines drank from a random well that turned out to be contaminated and had to retire.

American runner Thomas Hicks was given toxic stimulants, brandy, and egg whites to keep him going. He hallucinated while running and was helped by his team to cross the finish line first.

The 1904 Olympic Marathon brought about significant changes in Olympic regulations, including standardized regulations and high-quality facilities for future games. The controversies led to strict enforcement of rules for future races and the formation of the International Association of Athletics Federations. The infamy of this race also led the Olympic Committee to provide athletes with water and nourishment during marathons in subsequent years.

It's fascinating to note that the marathon started under a blazing sun with no water points until mile 12.5. The runners experienced hallucinations, exhaustion, and one even ate rotten apples from the side of the road. This race highlights the importance of ensuring proper conditions and ethical practices for the athletes' welfare and dignity.

Its legacy has seen great improvements in marathon safety and the development of standardized regulations globally. Its infamy has also hurled this Marathon to the forefront of Olympic history as one of the most memorable moments in the Games.

The Eruption of Mount Tambora

In the year 1815, something extraordinary occurred on the Indonesian island of Sumbawa. Mount Tambora, a notorious volcano located in the region, erupted in a historical explosion that would take the record books by storm. The eruption stretched across three days and left a catastrophic impact on the area, claiming the lives of thousands of people and devastating the region entirely.

Mount Tambora is found within the Ring of Fire – a region that spans across the Pacific Ocean and is infamous for its volcanic activity and earthquakes. Despite the history of volcanic eruptions in the area, none has ever been as powerful as the 1815 disaster that occurred on the mountain.

Interestingly, the eruption coincided with the Dutch East Indies period when the impact of the event left a significant mark on global trade and diplomacy.

Throughout the event, Mount Tambora's eruption consisted of several phases, including small earthquakes followed by ash and volcanic debris. Over the next few days, the volcano spewed countless amounts of rocks, ash, and molten lava. The ash traveled across the planet, all the way to Europe and North America, generating unexpected weather patterns. The impact was staggering that it was audible over a thousand miles away in Sumatra.

The eruption had immeasurable consequences, including tens of thousands of fatalities directly caused by the volcanic activity, famine, and disease outbreaks that followed subsequently. The eruption's impact saw a drop in global temperatures, leading to crop failures and food shortages all over the world, triggering a global food crisis, which lasted for many years.

Today, the catastrophic event left by Mount Tambora's eruption is remembered as a significant moment in world history, demonstrating the gravity of natural disasters and the importance of preparedness. The eruption also showed the world the catastrophic effects of climate change, with its impact still being felt across the globe today.

The mountain's caldera, created by the explosion, is now a popular tourist destination and serves as a vivid reminder of the spectacular eruption that once occurred.

The Year Without a Summer

In 1816, a strange and unsettling event occurred that would go down in history as the Year Without a Summer. It was a time of great upheaval in society, with colonial empires expanding, industrialization transforming economies, and political strife between world powers. This was a time when farmers were already worried about their crops due to unusual weather patterns, and little did they know that they were about to face a devastating blow.

Mount Tambora, located in Indonesia, erupted on April 5, 1815, releasing a staggering 160 cubic kilometers of debris into the atmosphere. The ash and gases that were spewed into the upper atmosphere enveloped the entire planet, resulting in a massive haze that reflected sunlight and dropped the temperature. The sudden climate disruption led to failed crops and starving livestock, causing widespread famine and outbreaks of disease.

The summer of 1816 brought sub-zero temperatures and snowfall to various parts of the world, causing rivers and lakes in Europe to freeze over and leaving people huddled around fires to keep warm. In the United States, New England experienced snowfall in the middle of June. The effects of the sudden temperature decrease were catastrophic, causing crop failures, food shortages, and economic instability.

The Year Without a Summer contributed immensely to society and culture. The famine and disease that resulted from the event caused mass migration to North America, and consequentially, inspired the development of new technologies and agricultural methods that would aid in mitigating the effects of future climate disruptions.

Interestingly, the Year Without a Summer also inspired some of the most iconic 19th century literary works, including Mary Shelley's Frankenstein and Lord Byron's poem, Darkness. Unfortunately, the event also contributed to the spread of cholera due to crowded and unsanitary living conditions that followed.

The scaled eruption of Mount Tambora is considered the most considerable volcanic occurrence in recorded history, and its devastating effects were felt worldwide for several years. It was an event that highlighted how vulnerable human societies are to sudden and unpredictable changes in the environment. The legacy of the event has, without a doubt, contributed to the development of climate science and the need for sustainable and resilient societies. It is a story that continues to inspire discussions on climate change and our collective pursuit of a better tomorrow.

The Great Leap Forward's Sparrow Campaign

The Great Leap Forward remains one of the most misguided social campaigns in history. China's Communist Party, under Mao Zedong's leadership, undertook the initiative between 1958 and 1962, attempting to modernize the country's agriculture. However, their policies had dire consequences, with one of the most infamous being the Sparrow Campaign.

At the time, China was an agrarian society, and with the government's new policies proving unpopular, they launched a propaganda campaign. This led to the Sparrow Campaign, which aimed to eradicate the birds as pests that consumed large quantities of grain. Citizens were encouraged to kill the birds by any means necessary, including destroying nests and eggs or scaring them off with pots and pans.

Unfortunately, like many Great Leap Forward policies, the Sparrow Campaign was misguided and lacked scientific backing. The event caused catastrophic ecological damage, with sparrows being an important part of the ecosystem. Their elimination led to a surge in insect populations, attracting locusts that consumed crops. This famine lasted from 1959 to1962 and resulted in the deaths of millions of people.

Interestingly, the campaign also had unintended consequences. Mao Zedong believed sparrows ate more grain than they were worth, and so called for their extermination. However, in their indiscriminate killing, millions of other birds, such as swallows, were also eliminated. Even sparrows living in urban areas, where they didn't pose a threat to agriculture, were targeted.

Today, the Great Leap Forward and the Sparrow Campaign are held up as examples of misguided policies and a lack of scientific knowledge. They stand as cautionary tales of how even well-meaning policies can have dire consequences when not based on scientific understanding.

In conclusion, the Sparrow Campaign remains one of history's most astonishingly catastrophic events. Its impact on the ecosystem, and the population of China was, severe. Its legacy reminds us of the importance of scientific knowledge when implementing policies and the potential costs of not having such information.

The Great Cat Massacre of Paris

In the mid-1700s, Paris was the center of printing and bookbinding, and cats were prevalent in the city streets as they kept rodents and pests away from the precious books.

But a group of printers harbored an irrational fear of the feline creatures, believing them to be witches' familiars that brought bad luck. Financial struggles and political tensions mixed with this superstition to create a mass killing of cats, resulting in the Great Cat Massacre of Paris.

The printers began their mission by targeting their own cats, convinced that the animals were hiding secret messages from their enemies. And then they expanded their mission, chasing every cat in sight through the city streets with sticks and rocks, eventually throwing them out of windows or hanging them in the streets. The killings continued until the streets were covered with the dead bodies of innocent cats.

The aftermath of the massacre was twofold. First, it resulted in a decrease in the population of cats, leading to an increase in the number of rats and other pests. Second, it sparked a new conversation about the dangers of superstition and irrational beliefs and the treatment of animals.

An interesting fact surrounding the Great Cat Massacre of Paris was that some printers believed the cats could talk and were conspiring against them. The printers were known for creating vulgar and satirical works of literature, and the killing of cats became a means of expressing their irreverence and contempt for authority.

Today the Great Cat Massacre of Paris is recognized as a senseless act of animal cruelty that serves as a warning of the dangers of superstition and mob mentality. It remains a lesson in the importance of valuing and respecting animals, and a reminder of how easily irrational beliefs can lead to tragic consequences. The event is still studied and discussed in universities worldwide, ensuring it will remain a part of history forever.

The Time it Rained Money in France

The Time It Rained Money: Montpellier's Legendary Moment of Hope
In the small town of Montpellier, France, something extraordinary occurred in 1948. On an otherwise sunny day, a shower of paper notes descended from the sky, much like snowflakes, and landed softly on the ground. This surreal occurrence, known as the Montpellier Shower or The Time It Rained Money, remains a legendary event that continues to capture imaginations around the globe.

To grasp the impact of this miraculous event, it's necessary to understand the context of what was happening in France at the time. The country was reeling from the aftermath of World War II, and strict currency controls made it difficult for citizens to access their money. Poverty, unemployment, and a severe economic crisis plagued the nation, and the summer of 1948 was hot and dry, exacerbating the situation.

On August 16, 1948, Montpellier experienced a miracle. Money began to fall from the sky, starting with small paper notes that swiftly turned into 100, 500, and 1,000-franc bills. Aircraft flew overhead and dropped wads of cash that exploded like confetti on the ground. People rushed out of their homes onto the streets, collecting the bills and running back home, eager to share their newfound wealth with their loved ones.

The French authorities were initially baffled and didn't know where the aircraft came from. It was later discovered that US Air Force planes were flying from Frankfurt to Naples and accidentally spilled their cargo over Montpellier.

At first, Montpellier's residents were elated and euphoric, but the event's consequences were mixed. The shower led to a considerable rise in consumer prices, inflation, and a wave of bank account withdrawals, prompting the government to take severe measures to stabilize the economy.

Interestingly, the total value of the dropped money was around 100 million francs, and only half of the cash that fell from the sky was ever recovered. The Montpellier shower even inspired a French movie, "L'argent tombe du ciel" (Money drops from the sky), in 1964.

Even decades later, The Time It Rained Money remains a captivating event that inspires wonder. It's a surreal moment that reminds us of the incredible power of hope and the dangers of sudden wealth. The event left an indelible mark on Montpellier and the world at large.

The Poe Toaster Mystery

The Poe Toaster Mystery is a strange and captivating event that happened annually for over 70 years. On January 19th, the birthday of famous American author Edgar Allan Poe, an unknown figure dressed completely in black would grace his grave in Baltimore, Maryland. The figure would place three red roses and a bottle of cognac at the site of the grave, before disappearing into the night. This mysterious character was identified as the Poe Toaster, and the event continued until 2010, without disclosing any reason for the tradition's termination.

Edgar Allan Poe was born in 1809 in Boston, Massachusetts, but spent many years in Baltimore, Maryland, where he become a celebrated writer of horror and gothic fiction. Poe wrote several memorable stories like "The Raven" and "The Tell-Tale Heart," which have become classics of American literature. After his demise in 1849, he was buried in a modest grave in Baltimore, where years later, a monument was erected in his honor.

The Poe Toaster Mystery began in the 1930s after a mysterious figure began visiting Poe's grave. The Poe Toaster was first sighted and reported in 1949, exactly 100 years after Poe's death. Since then, on the day of his birth every year, the Poe Toaster visits the grave site with three red roses and half-empty cognac. Nobody was ever able to identify the Poe Toaster's identity, despite several theories being put forward about the figure's person. Other people speculated that the Poe Toaster could be a family tradition that was handed down from generation to generation.

The Poe Toaster Mystery has captured the public's imagination and has become a part of Baltimore's cultural heritage. Many works of art, such as The Simpsons, have been inspired by this strange annual ritual, and it has become a tourist attraction. When the Poe Toaster did not show up in 2010, fans were disappointed and decided to continue the tradition by visiting Poe's grave site.

One of the most fascinating facts about the Poe Toaster is that the roses used every year were "French Burgundy," a variety that is rare and difficult to find. Another compelling fact is that the Poe Toaster always used a silver tipped cane, engraved with Poe's name, to toast the grave.

To this day, the Poe Toaster Mystery remains a fascinating part of Edgar Allan Poe's legacy. Some individuals still visit his grave on his birthday to honor his memory, and fans eagerly wait to see if the Poe Toaster will ever return. The identity of the Poe Toaster will always be a mystery, but it has transformed into a lasting legacy in honor of one of America's greatest authors.

The Demon Core Incidents

The Demon Core Incidents are a tragic reminder of the dangers of working with nuclear materials. These criticality accidents occurred at the Los Alamos National Laboratory in New Mexico during the development of nuclear weapons in 1945 and 1946. Scientists were working with a subcritical mass of plutonium, known as the "Demon Core," which had the potential to cause a criticality accident if mishandled. The inadvertent exposure to ionizing radiation would result in a devastating outcome.

On August 21, 1945, Harry K. Daghlian, Jr., a physicist working on the Demon Core, caused it to go critical when he accidentally dropped a tungsten carbide brick onto the core during an experiment. He made several attempts to remove the brick and stop the reaction, but it was too late. He received a high dose of radiation and died 25 days later.

Less than a year later, another physicist, Louis Slotin, was conducting an experiment on May 21, 1946, when he held two hemispheres of beryllium around the core with a screwdriver. The screwdriver slipped, causing the hemispheres to come too close together and the core to go critical. Slotin quickly removed the hemispheres, saving the lives of several others who were present, but he received a high dose of radiation and died nine days later.

The consequences of the Demon Core Incidents were significant. Stricter regulations and safety measures were implemented, and awareness of the dangers of ionizing radiation was raised. The accidents had a personal impact on the families and colleagues of the scientists involved, and emphasized the risks inherent in scientific research and development.

The Demon Core was involved in several nuclear weapons tests, including the Trinity test, which was the first successful test of an atomic bomb. The accidents involving the Demon Core were among the first documented criticality accidents in history. The exact mass of the Demon Core remains unknown, as it was never weighed before or after the accidents.

The Demon Core Incidents continue to be studied and remembered as important events in the history of nuclear weapons development and safety. They serve as a cautionary tale about the importance of strict safety protocols and proper training in scientific research, and the dangers of ionizing radiation.

The Exploding Whale of Florence, Oregon

In the quiet, coastal town of Florence, Oregon, the arrival of a 45-foot-long, 8-ton dead whale posed a safety risk to the community. To dispose of the rotting carcass, local officials made a fateful decision that would lead to an unexpected event: the "Exploding Whale".

With limited infrastructure, the authorities turned to the Oregon Highway Division and the US Navy for help. The solution they came up with was half a ton of dynamite to blow up the whale. Crowds gathered on the beach, eagerly awaiting the spectacle. However, what followed was a disaster beyond anyone's imagination.

As the dynamite exploded, the whale erupted into a shower of blubber and debris that rained down upon the beach and surrounding areas. The explosion damaged cars and buildings, leaving behind a gruesome smell and sight that lingered for days.

The event sparked immediate outrage and criticism from the public and media. The environmental and health impacts further exacerbated the situation. The explosion polluted the beach and exposed people to toxic whale blubber, causing long-term damage to the environment.

Despite the chaos, the exploding whale became a cultural phenomenon. The event has inspired songs, videos, cartoons, and memes, and even led the way in scientific research on disposing of whale carcasses.

Two fascinating facts surround the incident. Firstly, the explosion did not completely dispose of the whale carcass, but rather scattered its remains into small pieces that had to be later removed using heavy machinery and incinerators. Secondly, the explosion became popular in early 2000s internet culture, as a news video of it went viral and was widely shared online.

The "Exploding Whale" might have caused chaos in its time, but today, it is celebrated as an icon of Pacific Northwest humor and quirkiness. It serves as a reminder of the importance of environmental responsibility, and visitors still flock to Florence, Oregon, to see the remains of the infamous event.

The Great Train Wreck of 1918

The Great Train Wreck of 1918 is a moment in history that has remained etched in the minds of many Americans. On July 9th of that year, two passenger trains collided head-on outside Nashville, Tennessee. This tragic incident resulted in the deaths of 101 people, and over 170 others were left injured. The event was so disastrous that it came to be known as the deadliest train accident in American history.

During the trenches of World War I, the demand for transportation was at an all-time high, and the resources were limited. To accommodate the increased traffic, the Nashville, Chattanooga and St. Louis Railway Company implemented a new system that allowed for less frequent train inspections. However, this led to increased risk of accidents, a risk that, unfortunately, materialized.

On that fateful day, the westbound No. 4 train was scheduled to make a stop in Nashville, while the eastbound No. 1 train was meant to pass without stopping. But due to miscommunication, both trains ended up on the same track, resulting in a deadly collision at a speed of 50 miles per hour. The collision was so brutal that the steam engines piled up on top of each other, resulting in the flinging off of several train cars off the tracks.

The immediate aftermath was chaotic, with rescuers having to dig through the wreckage to search for survivors. The tragedy had far-reaching consequences, leading to new safety regulations regarding train travel. Besides, it left a lasting impact on the local community, with many families grieving the loss of loved ones. To honor the victims, a monument was erected in Nashville's Mount Olivet Cemetery, and annual memorial services are still held to this day.

Fascinating facts learned from the Great Train Wreck of 1918 include the survival of engineer J. T. Edwards, who suffered a broken arm and leg, and passenger Sam H. McKnight, who was found in the wreckage clutching onto a telephone.

As tragic as the accident was, it sparked changes that continue to shape society today. It serves as a reminder of the importance of safety regulations and proper communication. The Great Train Wreck of 1918 remains a significant moment in American history.

The Max Headroom Signal Hijacking

In the midst of technological advancements, political turmoil, and cultural change, America experienced a strange, unsettling event in November 1987. The Max Headroom Signal Hijacking - an infamous and mysterious incident - took place in Chicago, Illinois. For nearly two minutes, an eerie and surreal message took over two television stations, broadcasting from an unknown culprit wearing a mask of the popular fictional character Max Headroom. Viewers were left puzzled, and authorities were left scrambling to identify the culprit.

At the time, television had immense power and influence on the collective imagination and identity of Americans, making this event all the more alarming. Chicago, in particular, was home to major TV networks, studios, and personalities. On the evening of November 22nd, 1987, while airing an episode of "Doctor Who," local TV station WGN Channel 9's transmission was interrupted by a distorted image of a person in a Max Headroom mask. The hijacker mocked the show's cast, improvising nonsensical jokes, before the transmission was abruptly stopped. A few hours later, a similar message appeared on another Chicago TV station, WTTW Channel 11, with a cryptic and disturbing monologue that lasted over a minute. No one was able to identify the hijacker, leaving authorities to launch a fruitless investigation and stoke fears about television's vulnerability to outside interference.

The Max Headroom Signal Hijacking became a cultural legend, inspiring countless theories, hoaxes, and copycats. It raised serious questions about the reliance on technology for communication and the power of symbols in shaping perceptions and challenging authority. It also led to new security measures and regulations in the broadcasting industry. No one has ever discovered the identity of the hijacker, leaving the incident as a mysterious, unsolved crime that continues to fascinate and mystify people.

The incident sparked widespread interest and fascination, inspiring a 2015 documentary film called "The Max Headroom Incident." The character Max Headroom was initially created as a TV host and pitchman in the 1980s, known for its quirky personality and distinct visual appearance. The hijacker used a homemade transmitter to interfere with the TV signals, a feat that required technical skills and resources.

The Max Headroom Signal Hijacking is still considered a significant moment in TV history, emblematic of the 1980s zeitgeist and a symbol of resistance and subversion. In popular culture, it has been parodied and referenced multiple times, cementing its place in the cultural canon. The incident serves as a cautionary tale about the dangers of unchecked technology and the allure of spectacle - a reminder of the vulnerability of systems we take for granted.

The Night the Sky Rained Sea Creatures in California

On a dark and cloudy night on October 18, 1865, the sky showered Santa Monica, California with a bizarre and unexpected sight. Thousands of tiny marine creatures, known as salps, began falling from the sky, covering everything in slimy and transparent coatings. The incident left those who witnessed it in awe and disbelief.

The area had a reputation for erratic weather patterns, including droughts, fires, and occasional floods. Droughts had been ravaging the area leading up to the event, and it's believed that a heavy rainstorm disrupted a group of salps that were floating offshore. The environmental instability caused the creatures to rain from the sky.

The rain of salps has been described as a wonderland of mysterious maritime organisms. They were transparent and measured around two to three inches in size. Some locals thought they were tiny fish, while others believed them to be jellyfish.

While the incident had little impact on society, it fascinated the scientific community and sparked discussions about the possibility of salps reproducing in the sky. The creatures didn't pose any significant threat to humans, and they were disposed of sustainably. The event paved the way for a broader study in meteorological phenomena.

It's uncommon for salps to thrive outside the marine environment or rain from the sky. Some speculate that waterspouts may have played a role in lifting the creatures from the ocean. However, there is no empirical proof to support this theory.

The incident remains a curious anecdote for the small coastal community in California. It serves as a reminder of the natural world's unpredictability, the infinite possibilities that lie beyond our comprehension. While the salps' rain didn't leave a lasting legacy, it continues to spark curiosity among researchers seeking a better understanding of nature's aberrations.

The Silent Parade of 1917

In the early 1900s, black Americans migrated from the South to Northern cities seeking better work opportunities and an escape from segregation, but instead found harassment, violence, and discrimination. In response, civil rights organizations like the National Association for the Advancement of Colored People (NAACP) were formed to combat this injustice and fight for equal rights.

One of the most notable events organized by the NAACP was The Silent Parade of 1917, a march that took place on July 28th in New York City. Thousands of people, all dressed in white and carrying signs demanding an end to racial violence and equal rights before the law, peacefully walked through the streets. The parade was led by civil rights icons like W.E.B. Du Bois and Arthur Spingarn, and ended with speeches at Madison Square.

Despite the peaceful nature of the event, some in the crowd were hostile and violent towards the marchers, throwing rocks and bottles and leading to several arrests. The Silent Parade was nevertheless a significant moment in the history of civil rights, drawing national attention to the issue of racial discrimination and inspiring future campaigns for equality.

It also helped to set the stage for the March on Washington in 1963, and other major protests that brought about significant changes in American society.

The impact of The Silent Parade was both immediate and long-lasting. It garnered sympathy and support from white Americans and put pressure on President Woodrow Wilson to take action against racism. The parade also inspired a popular anthem for the civil rights movement, "Silent Parade," composed by African American musician Charley Johnson.

While often overlooked in mainstream histories of the civil rights movement, The Silent Parade of 1917 remains a crucial event that inspired generations of activists to stand up against discrimination and fight for the cause of racial equality. It serves as a powerful reminder of the importance of peaceful protest and the progress that can be made when people come together to demand change.

The Cleveland Balloon Disaster

In 1986, Pepsi-Cola planned a promotional event that would end in a tragedy nobody could have foreseen. The event was set to showcase a team of skydivers that would take the leap from seven helium-filled balloons at an altitude of 3,000 feet. The plan was to create a unique spectacle that would capture the attention of the public, but things went terribly wrong.

The Cleveland Balloon Disaster occurred on May 30, 1986, during the Memorial Day weekend, which was set aside to honor fallen soldiers. The location was chosen because of its proximity to the Pepsi-Cola headquarters in New York City and the city's accessibility to the public. Cleveland was known for its sporting events, and it was thought that the event would attract a large crowd.

The ill-fated event began with four skydivers taking the leap from the balloons, but suddenly, three of the balloons got caught in a wind change, and their tethers snapped. The balloons were carried towards Lake Erie, dragging the divers with them. One of the balloons crashed into a building, killing two of the skydivers on the spot. The third skydiver got entangled in the balloon's rigging and fell to his death. The fourth skydiver managed to untangle himself and landed in Lake Erie, where he was rescued by a U.S. Coast Guard helicopter.

The aftermath of the disaster prompted an investigation into the safety standards of promotional events, and it was discovered that the event had not complied with the Federal Aviation Administration (FAA) regulations. Pepsi-Cola was fined $1.5 million for their role in the tragedy, and they paid compensation to the families of the victims. The event became a wake-up call for the need for proper safety protocols for all such events.

The immediate impact of the tragedy led to the creation of new regulations that required mandatory safety checks, inspections, and compliance with FAA regulations. The footage of the event was later used in court proceedings. The Cleveland Balloon Disaster serves as a reminder that safety should always be a top priority during such events.

Reliving the tragic event leaves many spectators traumatized to this day. It is still remembered as one of the worst tragedies in the history of promotional events. The seasoned skydivers who lost their lives between them had over 100,000 skydives. Lessons learned from the disaster continue to remain relevant, and safety standards are continually reviewed, ensuring that safety comes first.

The Great Fire of Smyrna

In the early 20th century, the bustling city of Smyrna (now known as Izmir), was a melting pot of different cultures and religions. Greeks, Turks, Jews, Armenians, and other minority groups called the city home, living together in harmony in this cosmopolitan hub of trade and commerce. However, the Ottoman Empire had been in decline for years and by 1920, Smyrna, or as it was then known, İzmir, was handed over to Greece under the Treaty of Sevres.

This sparked tension between the Greeks and Turkish nationalists and hostilities erupted in the city. By August 1922, the Turkish nationalists, led by Mustafa Kemal Ataturk, launched a campaign that saw them successfully expel Greek forces from Anatolia. As the Greek army retreated towards Smyrna, tens of thousands of Greek and Armenian refugees also arrived in the city, hoping to find safety from the advancing Turkish forces.

However, tensions were already running high between nationalist Turks and Greeks, and on September 13th, a fire broke out in the Armenian quarter of the city. Fueled by high winds and flammable materials, the fire quickly spread, burning for days. Meanwhile, Greek and Armenian residents were trapped in the burning city, whilst Turkish nationalists prevented international aid from reaching Smyrna. Despite the Allied forces being stationed nearby, they were unable to intervene, and many ships refused to take in refugees due to fear of riots and violence.

The fire eventually burnt itself out, but not before thousands of people had lost their lives and many more had been displaced, losing their homes and possessions. The event, known as the Great Fire of Smyrna, marked the downfall of the Ottoman Empire and the birth of Turkish nationalism under Ataturk. It had a profound impact, not just on the city and its residents, but on relations between Greece and Turkey, leading to continuing tensions and disputes over the years.

Although the cause of the fire is unknown (some say it was started by a cigarette or a pipe in a Turkish or Armenian home), it was so intense that it could be seen from ships in the Aegean Sea, over 20 miles away. The fire has also been immortalized in the works of famous writers such as Ernest Hemingway and John Dos Passos.

The Great Fire of Smyrna remains a symbol of the dangers of nationalism, sectarianism, and war, and its lessons continue to resonate in the modern world. It is a tragic event in the history of Turkey and the region, one that has inspired numerous books, documentaries, and artistic works.

The Comet That Sparked a Panic (Halley's Comet in 1910)

Halley's Comet: A Tale of Superstition and Scientific Discovery

In 1910, the world was gripped by panic and terror as Halley's Comet made its way across the sky. The comet's tail was thought to contain poisonous gases that would end all life on Earth, and religious leaders claimed it was a sign of the world's end. Some cities even shut down schools and businesses. However, the predicted doomsday scenario did not happen, and the comet passed without incident.

Despite the advancement of science and technology, Halley's Comet was still considered a mystic and foreboding omen. The 1910 visit was significant because it was the first time scientists were capable of analyzing the comet up close. Despite scientists' rational explanations, superstition, and fear continued to plague the comet's appearance.

Misinformation and rumors became prevalent leading up to the comet's arrival, causing public hysteria. People believed that the comet's tail contained deadly cyanogen gas, which would poison the Earth's atmosphere, and that the electrically charged tail would cause wildfires and earthquakes. When the comet became visible, people took drastic measures to protect themselves, barricading themselves inside their homes or wearing gas masks. Some fled to rural regions in hopes of escaping the threat, and schools and businesses were closed to prevent panic.

Despite the hysteria, the comet's appearance also inspired wonder and amazement, allowing astronomers to examine its composition and trajectory, leading to significant discoveries about comets.

The panic over Halley's Comet highlighted the potential dangers of misinformation and the importance of scientific communication. The event sparked a renewed curiosity in astronomy, contributing significantly to our comprehension of comets and motivating subsequent space exploration.

Today, Halley's Comet remains a compelling link to curiosity and wonder, embraced by scientists and stargazers every 76 years. The event is a significant moment in astronomy's history, emphasizing the importance of precise, accurate, and efficient scientific communication.

The Lake Nyos Disaster

In Cameroon in 1986, a beautiful volcanic lake called Lake Nyos became the site of an unthinkable disaster. Over the centuries, under the peaceful waters of the lake, chambers of magma had been emitting carbon dioxide gas. Small releases had occurred before, but nothing like the cloud that was to come on August 21st.

As a result of an enormous release of CO2, a deadly cloud spread over the surrounding villages, killing 1,700 people and 3,500 animals. The weight of the CO2 was so heavy that it suffocated its victims by displacing the air in their lungs, leading to a simultaneous and sudden death. It was initially thought to be a chemical attack, and it took some time before rescue teams identified the cause.

When rescue teams arrived the following day, they found the area covered in white dust, with trees and plants standing discolored or stripped bare by the gas. The disaster was so abrupt that there was no warning or escape once it began.

The long-term consequences of the Lake Nyos disaster had a significant impact on the environment and wildlife, with farming in the nearby area set back for years, and nearby schools closed and with declining attendance. After the event, degassing of Lake Nyos began with the installation of pipes for the purpose.

Scientists estimate that the cloud was equivalent to the amount of carbon dioxide released by humans in a city of one million people over an entire year. The event was so devastating that in some towns, up to 25% of the population died.

Today, the Lake Nyos disaster remains a tragic ecological event that serves as a lesson about the dangers of volcanic gas. Crater lake monitoring and warning have become a significant issue for nations worldwide, with scientists continuing their research into the cause of the disaster and developing advanced techniques for degassing lakes.

The Moonlight Murders of Texarkana

In the sleepy town of Texarkana, life was quiet and idyllic. That was until the Moonlight Murders of 1946, which shook the town to its core. Young couples parked in isolated spots were targeted by the unknown assailant who roamed the streets at night, his face concealed by a white mask with holes cut out for eyes. His weapon of choice? A pistol, which he used to smash car windows before beating and shooting his victims.

Over six weeks he struck five times, claiming the lives of five people and injuring three others. Law enforcement issued warnings, but the attacker went undetected. Dubbed the 'Phantom Killer,' the assailant disappeared as quickly as he appeared, leaving the townsfolk terrified and on edge.

The impact of the murders was felt long after the killer vanished. Many people moved from the town, its reputation forever tarnished. The case prompted changes in law enforcement practices, as investigators turned to forensic evidence.

Despite over 4000 tips and leads, and one particularly curious tip from a psychic veteran, the case was never solved.

Today, the Moonlight Murders are a popular topic in popular culture, inspiring books, movies, and shows that explore the unsolved mystery of Texarkana. Though the town has moved on from the murders, the tragedy still resonates with people today.

The killer's identity remains a mystery, and his legacy lives on, haunting the town and its people all these years later.

The Sinking of the SS Eastland

The SS Eastland sinking on the Chicago River on July 24th, 1915, remains one of the most devastating maritime disasters in the history of the Great Lakes. The Eastland was carrying over 2,500 passengers, mostly employees and their families of the Western Electric Company, on an annual chartered excursion to Michigan City, Indiana.

The passengers boarded the ship, but it became alarmingly tilty and top-heavy, with the crew loading the boat unevenly. Crew members warned passengers about instability issues, but the message went unheeded, and the passengers continued to board the ship anyway. Suddenly, without warning, the ship tipped over on one side, trapping hundreds of people underneath it.

The Chicago Fire Department was quick to respond, but the swift currents of the river made the rescue effort almost impossible, causing a death toll of 844 people, including 22 families.

The aftermath of the disaster left the entire city of Chicago in shock, with additional morticians brought in from neighboring towns to manage the overwhelming death toll. Funeral homes all over the city had to be used to accommodate the loss of life. A memorial, shaped like an angel statue, was later erected to commemorate the victims.

The disaster had a significant impact on the regulation of maritime safety standards. The Seaman's Act of 1915 was introduced, mandating stricter regulations for passenger ships to prevent similar accidents from occurring. The sinking of the SS Eastland became a catalyst for the creation of the first US Coast Guard lifeboat stations located on Lake Michigan.

The tragedy has since been viewed as a reminder of the critical importance of safety in all aspects of life, motivating the implementation of improved safety standards throughout various industrial sectors. Today, the location of the disaster stands as a haunting reminder of the human cost of negligence and inadequate safety standards.

The Salish Sea Human Foot Discoveries

The Salish Sea: 21 Human Feet Washed Ashore

The Salish Sea, located between British Columbia and Washington state, is renowned for its ferocious tides and powerful currents - capable of carrying even the heaviest of objects miles away. Indigenous communities have called it home for thousands of years, with a rich cultural heritage. In the 19th century, European explorers, fur traders, and settlers established towns along its shores. But, in recent years, the Salish Sea has become a site of tragedy.

The first foot was discovered in August 2007, on a beach near Vancouver Island. A right foot wearing a shoe - it sparked widespread speculation about the person's identity and cause of death. Over the following years, more feet were found; intertidal waters yielding their secrets as they washed up on the shores. Investigators identified most as those who'd died in accidents or suicides, but some cases remain unsolved.

While the discoveries have been tragic for families and communities involved, there is one bright spot. They've also raised awareness of forensic science and the importance of DNA analysis in solving crimes. Additionally, the discoveries have led to conversations about the growing issue of missing and murdered indigenous women in Canada, resulting in changes in policing policies and initiatives to address the problem.

This topic never ceases to fascinate. One of the foot discoveries was later discovered to have been a hoax - a fake foot stuffed inside a running shoe and left on a beach as a practical joke. And, due to the strong tides and currents of Salish Sea, feet have been found in both US and Canadian waters.

The Salish Sea human foot discoveries remain a topic of fixation, inspiring theories and musings on their meaning and origin. Authorities continue to investigate any new revelations, while raising awareness about the importance of water safety. With the Salish Sea's powerful forces and deep mysteries, it's clear that we've not heard the last of this, one of the most incredible events to have ever occurred.

The Goiânia Accident

The Goiânia Accident: A Tragic Reminder of the Importance of Safety Protocols

In September 1987, a shocking event occurred in Goiânia, Brazil. A metallic object, which turned out to be a radiotherapy machine containing the highly radioactive substance cesium-137, was found in an abandoned hospital. The ensuing events were even more alarming, as the cesium-137 was released into the environment, exposing over 250 people to it. This incident, known as the Goiânia Accident, is considered one of the worst radiation accidents in history, resulting in four deaths and numerous cases of radiation sickness.

At the time of the accident, Brazil was undergoing a transition from a military dictatorship to a democratic government. It was also modernizing its industrial and technological infrastructure and making progress in medical advancements such as the use of radiotherapy for cancer treatment. These factors contributed to the perfect storm that led to the Goiânia Accident.

Two men dismantled the radiotherapy machine and took the glowing blue powder inside to show off to their friends and family. Unwittingly, they spread the radioactive material to various locations throughout the city, causing widespread exposure. Those who came into contact with the substance suffered physical symptoms such as vomiting, hair loss, and skin burns. The Brazilian Nuclear Energy Commission quickly arrived to contain the radiation, but four people died as a direct result of exposure, and many others suffered long-term illnesses.

The Goiânia Accident prompted the Brazilian government to strengthen regulations and safety measures for handling radioactive materials and to raise awareness of the potential hazards of disused radioactive sources. It also sparked international discussions about the need for proper management and disposal of such materials. Today, scientists are still studying the long-term effects of radiation exposure on people and the environment.

The Goiânia Accident has inspired a variety of creative works, including a novel, a play, and films. Parts of Goiânia had to be dismantled and rebuilt due to the severity of the radioactive contamination in the city.

This tragic event serves as a reminder of the importance of proper safety protocols when handling hazardous materials. It has also become a case study for nuclear researchers, medical professionals, and regulators, highlighting the potential dangers of nuclear accidents and the significance of public communication and education regarding radiation risks. Ultimately, the Goiânia Accident changed the way the world thinks about radioactive materials and their safe handling.

The Boston Molassacre

On a sunny afternoon in Boston's North End neighborhood, something horrific happened that no one could have ever imagined. It was January 15, 1919, and the United States had just reached the height of its prohibition era, where alcohol consumption and production were strictly prohibited. That day, a catastrophic event occurred that would go down in history as one of America's deadliest industrial accidents – the Boston Molassacre.

The incident took place at the Purity Distilling Company, a subsidiary of United States Industrial Alcohol (USIA), which produced rum from molasses. 2.3 million gallons of molasses were held in a poorly constructed steel tank, which was not equipped to manage such a heavy load. Due to this negligence, a loud bang was heard that day, and the 50-foot high steel tank exploded, releasing torrents of sticky brown syrup through the streets that trapped and drowned people and horses on its path.

The aftermath was devastating, with 21 people, including children, losing their lives, and over 150 people sustaining injuries. Buildings and streets were destroyed, and it took several days to clean up the sticky mess. The disaster caused damages estimated to be worth $1,000,000 in today's currency.

The incident resulted in massive lawsuits against USIA, and more than 300 claimants filed lawsuits against the company, seeking compensation. Unfortunately, the claimants did not receive compensation until almost six years later, in 1925.

Beyond the tragedies and losses, we can draw some fascinating facts from this catastrophic event. Within seconds of the blast, the molasses flow was so devastating that it reached over a mile-long in breadth. The disaster also left some survivors haunted, with lifelong psychological scars.

The Boston Molassacre remains a reminder of the importance of prioritizing safety and the need to take necessary measures to prevent such catastrophic accidents. At the same time, the disaster led to the creation of stricter safety regulations and codes to prevent similar accidents in the future. Today, it is remembered as a preventable disaster caused by corporate negligence and a tragedy that shook a community and a nation. It emphasizes that in every action, especially ones with considerable consequences, accountability, responsibility, and safety are vital.

The 1962 Alcatraz Escape

The 1962 Alcatraz Escape, considered one of the most incredible prison breaks, is a legendary tale of three convicts, Frank Morris, Clarence Anglin, and John Anglin. The escape happened on June 11, 1962, in San Francisco Bay, California, at the Alcatraz Federal Penitentiary, which held some of the most dangerous criminals in the United States at the time. Known for its security and isolation, Alcatraz was situated on a small, rocky island, making it almost impossible to escape, and even earned the reputation of being escape-proof. Yet, despite the reputation, prisoners had attempted to escape in the past, but with no success.

On the fateful night of June 11, 1962, Morris, Clarence, and John made their daring escape from their cells. The trio had spent months creating false walls in their cells, using stolen materials such as spoons and saw blades. The men also created life-sized dummies to lay in their beds as decoys during headcount. Cleverly, the three prisoners managed to reach the roof of the prison, sneaking down a ventilation shaft to reach the ground level. Stealing rafts made of waterproof raincoats and paddles made of scrap wood, they embarked on a long and treacherous journey across the bay's currents, taking them to the mainland, where they vanished without a trace.

The FBI launched a massive manhunt to locate the fugitives, but their search proved futile, and no evidence of the prisoners' death was found. Many people still believe that they may have successfully hidden and lived out the rest of their lives covertly, yet the fate of the inmates remains, in large part, a mystery.

The Alcatraz Escape marked a significant moment in the history of American prisons. It showed that even the most formidable prison systems could fail when challenges by resourceful prisoners. As such, the government closed down the Alcatraz prison in 1963, and it has remained open for tourists ever since.

The Alcatraz Escape has continued to capture the imagination of people all around the world, inspiring books, movies, and TV series, including the timeless classic, "Escape from Alcatraz," starring Clint Eastwood. Thanks to the FBI's continued interest in the case, new evidence and leads resurface every few years, keeping the legend of the Alcatraz escapees alive.

Some fascinating facts contribute to the legend, as it is believed that the men could have created papier-mâché heads to act as decoys, inspiring many stories and tales. Modern perceptions of the events that happened at the Alcatraz prison remain incredibly captivating, and the escapees have become legends, with some people still claiming that they are still alive today.

The Hindenburg Disaster

In 1937, the mighty LZ 129 Hindenburg, pride and joy of the Zeppelin Company, made its way across the Atlantic. This behemoth of an airship was over 800 feet long, and it carried passengers in the lap of luxury between Germany and the United States. However, tensions between the two countries were running high, and political events leading up to World War II hung heavy in the air.

On May 6, 1937, the Hindenburg came in to dock at the Naval Air Station in Lakehurst, New Jersey. But as the airship was being secured to the mooring mast, disaster struck. Flames burst forth from the tail section, and within seconds, the massive airship was engulfed in fire. Crew and passengers alike scrambled to flee the inferno, but for 36 people, it was too late. The world looked on in horror as the Hindenburg Disaster unfolded, captured on film and radio for all to see.

The results of the tragedy were far-reaching. Airships had been the epitome of luxurious travel, but the Hindenburg Disaster shattered that illusion forever. The aviation industry saw a sudden upsurge in the development of commercial aviation, as people realized that airships simply weren't safe. The disaster also left a profound mark on public perception of technology and fear of travel in general. Internationally, relations between Germany and the United States were strained even further.

Today, the Hindenburg Disaster remains a fascinating and cautionary tale. The disaster was not the first of its kind, but it was certainly the deadliest. The Hindenburg had been scheduled to receive helium in Frankfurt, but for political reasons, it was forced to use the highly-flammable hydrogen instead. Conspiracy theories arose, suggesting everything from sabotage by Nazis to a lightning strike as the cause of the disaster.

Modern air travel has evolved since the days of the Hindenburg, but the disaster remains fixed in our minds as a symbol of the risks inherent in technological advancement. Books, documentaries, and even films continue to memorialize the Hindenburg, like the classic film "Hindenburg" starring George C. Scott. The legacy of the disaster reminds us of the importance of safety in innovation.

The Patterson-Gimlin Bigfoot Film

The Patterson-Gimlin Bigfoot Film is a captivating 59-second clip that shows a mysterious creature known as Bigfoot traversing through a wooded area in Bluff Creek, California. The film was shot in October of 1967 by two aspiring filmmakers, Roger Patterson and Bob Gimlin, who claimed to have stumbled upon the creature while on horseback.

Bigfoot, also known as Sasquatch, is a fabled figure that has intrigued people worldwide for centuries. In North America, where its sightings have been mostly documented, many claim to have seen the creature, albeit without conclusive evidence.

On October 20, 1967, Patterson and Gimlin were capturing footage of the area's wildlife when they caught sight of the creature. The duo got off their horses and followed Bigfoot on foot, camera in hand. Patterson captured footage of the creature as it strided through the woods away from them, briefly turning back to face the camera before disappearing from sight.

The Patterson-Gimlin Bigfoot Film gained widespread media attention, with people split over whether it was real or a hoax. The footage had a significant impact both on popular culture and Bigfoot research. Expert opinion on the footage authenticity was divided, with no conclusive proof discovered either way.

Despite the mystery surrounding the footage, the Patterson-Gimlin Bigfoot Film has cemented its place in pop culture ubiquitously. The iconic image of the figure remains instantly recognizable to most people, providing a glimpse into the enduring mystery and fascination that people have with Bigfoot.

Today, Bigfoot remains a topic of interest, with continued debate and discussion among enthusiasts and researchers. While the Patterson-Gimlin Bigfoot Film has played an essential role in the creature's popularity, no definitive evidence of its existence has been found yet, which perpetuates the mystery.

The Great Los Angeles Air Raid

As the United States was still recuperating from the devastating attack on Pearl Harbor, on February 24, 1942, an event occurred over Los Angeles that became one of the most controversial and mysterious military incidents during World War II. Called the Great Los Angeles Air Raid, the event involved a barrage of anti-aircraft artillery fired at an unidentified object that was believed to be an enemy aircraft. The target's identity and purpose were never officially determined, which stirred much speculation and debate.

At the time, California was considered one of the most vulnerable locations for attack due to its proximity to the Pacific, numerous military bases, and industrial sites. This vulnerability caused the tension and anxiety in the area to rise, amplified by reports of Japanese submarines and spy activity along the coast and sightings of mysterious flying objects attributed to enemy aircraft or weather balloons.

The event began shortly after 2 a.m. on February 25 when air-raid sirens sounded throughout Los Angeles. Anti-aircraft batteries were activated and searchlights swept the skies looking for the supposed intruder. For over an hour, gunfire and explosions echoed through the city as tens of thousands of rounds were fired at the elusive object. Witnesses reported seeing glowing objects in the sky dodging the incoming rounds, while others said they'd seen planes hit and crashing to the ground. All told, despite the intensity and duration of the attack, no actual enemy aircraft or wreckage were ever found.

The military later claimed that the incident had been a case of "false alarm" triggered by "war nerves" and/or weather-related anomalies, such as a drifting weather balloon or a flock of birds. The Great Los Angeles Air Raid sparked panic and confusion amongst the residents of Los Angeles who had already been traumatized by the attack on Pearl Harbor. Authorities ordered a blackout, and thousands of people fled their homes and sought refuge in underground tunnels and basements.

The event raised questions about the reliability of military defense systems as well as the possibility of UFO and extraterrestrial activity. While the official explanation dismissed such speculation, conspiracy theories and alternative explanations have persisted to this day and have been featured in books and documentaries.

The Great Los Angeles Air Raid has become a cultural phenomenon, a reference in movies, TV shows, music, and literature as a symbol of the fear, uncertainty, and paranoia of wartime and its aftermath.

The London Monster

London had a big problem in the late 18th century: the notorious London Monster. He preyed upon young women, attacking them with a sharp object and leaving them traumatized and wounded. Panic swept the city as the police struggled to catch the perpetrator or find any useful clues.

Dubbed the "London Monster," this attacker terrorized London for several months between 1788 and 1790, at a time when women were considered vulnerable and the city had a reputation for high crime. It was a perfect storm for the emergence of this sinister figure.

The police initially had difficulty finding the culprit. Victims claimed he had been hideous and had attempted to mutilate their faces. Rumors spread, and the press sensationalized the attacks, making the public more nervous. However, the authorities eventually offered a reward for information, and a man named John Colley was arrested.

He had a reputation as an eccentric character around town and had previously been arrested on suspicion of burglary. Under torture, he admitted to these crimes, but there was no physical evidence linking him to them. Despite this, Colley was found guilty and sentenced to deportation.

The London Monster had a significant impact on the city, with young women becoming extremely cautious in their day-to-day lives. The police procedures that arose during the case were based on principles of civil policing that are still used by modern-day police departments. During his reign of terror, popular culture produced plays, songs, and literature in response to the public's fascination with the case.

One of the London Monster's victims was the aunt of famous writer Jane Austen. Colley's guilt has long been questioned, and recent investigations suggest he may have been falsely accused. The legacy of the London Monster is fascinating, as the case remains a classic example of historical criminology.

It highlights issues surrounding police brutality, criminal profiling, and forensic technology that still challenge the criminal justice system to this day. Although forgotten in modern times, the case remains a chilling reminder of how rumors and panic can grip society.

The Iron Mask Prisoner

In the late 17th century, the infamous Bastille prison in Paris was home to a mysterious prisoner, known as the Iron Mask Prisoner. This prisoner was notable for the mask made of iron that he wore, which kept his identity hidden from his captors and fellow inmates. Rumors and theories spread about his true identity, but to this day, nobody knows who he was or why he was imprisoned.

The Bastille was known for imprisoning political dissidents and writers who spoke out against the monarchy, and the Iron Mask Prisoner was no exception. He entered the Bastille in 1670, during the reign of King Louis XIV, a despotic ruler who presided over a kingdom beset with poverty, corruption, and social unrest. In this context, the prisoner's mystery took on mythical proportions, inspiring countless stories and legends over the years.

The true identity of the Iron Mask Prisoner remains a mystery to this day, despite numerous historians and researchers attempting to uncover his identity. He remained in the Bastille for over 30 years, living a confined and isolated life until his death in 1703.

His story has become a symbol of tyranny and oppression, influencing literature and cinema, including Alexandre Dumas' novel "The Man in the Iron Mask" and a 1998 film adaptation starring Leonardo DiCaprio.

Although theories abound about the Iron Mask Prisoner's true identity, there is little concrete evidence about his life before imprisonment. Some historians believe that he was a political prisoner, while others think he may have been a criminal or vagrant. The mask he wore was also unusual for the Bastille, leading some to speculate that he was a particularly important or dangerous prisoner.

The Iron Mask Prisoner's story lives on to this day, representing an enduring symbol of oppression and injustice. Although his true identity may never be known, his tale remains one of the most compelling and enigmatic in history.

The Villisca Axe Murders

In the quiet town of Villisca, Iowa, a grisly event shook the community to its core. On June 10th, 1912, the prosperous Moore family and their two young houseguests were brutally murdered with an axe while they were asleep in their beds. The shocking details of the case swept the nation, but despite numerous investigations and suspects, the killer was never identified, and the case remains unsolved to this day.

Villisca was a close-knit community, where everyone knew each other, and crime was rare. The Moores were well-respected and active members of their church and society. However, the social, economic, and political upheavals of the time, including labor unrest and the temperance movement, as well as the lingering effects of the Civil War, also affected the town.

The crime scene itself was chilling. The killer covered the victims' heads with sheets and the mirrors and windows with clothing, suggesting a ritualistic motive. The bodies were discovered by a concerned neighbor who grew worried when the family didn't show up for church. The aftermath was chaotic, with numerous suspects, false leads, and even national manhunts.

However, the Villisca Axe Murders had a significant impact on the town and the nation beyond the initial trauma. There was a surge in demand for home security measures, including locks, alarms, and guard dogs. The case also contributed to growing public awareness and concern about violent crime, and it was a turning point in the use of forensic science in criminal investigations.

Yet, what makes the Villisca Axe Murders truly fascinating is the bizarre aspects of the case. The killer reportedly stayed in the house for several hours after the crime, eating food from the Moores' kitchen, leaving behind a bowl of bloody water, and even a handwritten note on the wall. The case has inspired numerous books, films, and documentaries, with many modern-day amateur sleuths, armchair detectives, and conspiracy theorists, still trying to uncover new evidence and identify the killer.

As the case remains unsolved to this day, the legacy of the Villisca Axe Murders remains an enduring mystery and a cautionary tale about the limits of justice and the dangers of violence and obsession.

The Antikythera Mechanism Discovery

In the depths of the Aegean Sea lies a treasure that uncovered a partly-unknown facet of ancient Greek civilization. In 1901, a group of sponge divers were left in awe as they stumbled upon a strange bronze mechanism while off the coast of Antikythera in Greece. Later coined as the "Antikythera Mechanism," this intricate and mysterious object took the scientific community by storm, changing how we understand ancient Greek knowledge.

The Greeks were renowned for their scientific and technological advancements, particularly in astronomy and mechanics. However, it remained a mystery how they applied this knowledge to innovate new technologies. Upon inspection of the Antikythera Mechanism, scholars were astounded at the level of mechanical engineering the ancient Greeks possessed. The object featured dozens of gears, dials, and inscriptions written in Greek. It was an ancient analog computer designed to predict astronomical positions and the timing of solar eclipses.

The device is believed to date back to 150-100 BCE, making it over two thousand years old. When the Antikythera Mechanism was discovered, it revealed that the Greeks' mathematical and engineering knowledge was more advanced than previously imagined. This newfound insight into the complexity of ancient technology impacted modern-day astronomy and provided scholars with greater insight into our ancestors' view of the universe.

Initially, scholars dismissed the Antikythera Mechanism as an astrolabe or a navigational device until x-ray machines in the 1950s revealed its true complexity. The reconstruction of the device took over a decade of research and development as much of the original object was lost or broken.

Today, many scientists and researchers still study the mechanism to understand its true capabilities and its impact on ancient society. Its discovery remains an astonishing moment in scientific history and a testament to human innovation.

The Antikythera Mechanism has left a lasting legacy on both the scientific and cultural worlds. The device has become an icon of ancient knowledge, which sparked greater interest in ancient Greek technology. Its influence extends to modern-day mechanical engineering, inspiring new designs for modern astronomical technology.

The Galveston Hurricane of 1900

The Galveston Hurricane of 1900: A Tragedy and Its Legacy

In 1900, Galveston, Texas, was hit by the deadliest hurricane in US history. Despite being a thriving port city with a population of over 36,000, Galveston lacked adequate infrastructure to withstand the ferocity of a hurricane. The natural disaster claimed over 6,000 lives and destroyed much of the city.

The Galveston Hurricane formed in the Caribbean Sea, intensified rapidly, and hit Cuba before reaching Galveston. The storm had winds of 145 mph and caused storm surges of up to 15 feet. When the hurricane hit Galveston on September 8, it quickly destroyed over 3,600 homes and swept away buildings and ships. Many people were left stranded and clung to various objects in an attempt to escape the raging waters.

Isaac Cline, the chief meteorologist of the Galveston Weather Bureau, downplayed the potential impact of the storm, but he lost his wife and unborn child in the hurricane.

The aftermath of the Galveston Hurricane was catastrophic, with many bodies lining the streets and survivors struggling to find basic necessities like food, water, and shelter.

The disaster prompted a massive relief effort, with volunteers and aid organizations rushing to Galveston to provide assistance. However, the city's recovery was slow and painful, with many residents leaving for other parts of the country and the economy suffering a significant setback.

The Galveston Hurricane of 1900 was a turning point in hurricane forecasting, preparedness, and emergency response. It led to extensive debates and discussions on these topics, resulting in innovations in storm tracking, weather monitoring, and flood control measures. Galveston underwent massive engineering projects to prevent future vulnerability to hurricanes.

Today, Galveston commemorates the disaster through an annual hurricane commemoration event and several historical landmarks, museums, and memorials. The hurricane is a reminder of the resilience and strength of the human spirit in the face of natural disasters and the importance of preparedness, planning, and community solidarity in times of crisis.

The Collyer Brothers' Hoard

In the mid-20th century, New York City witnessed one of the most bizarre cases of hoarding in modern history, The Collyer Brothers' Hoard. The two brothers, Langley and Homer, hailed from a wealthy family and were highly educated. Langley was an engineer who graduated from Columbia University, while Homer was a gifted pianist who studied at the Paris Conservatory. However, after their parents passed away, the brothers became eccentric recluses, living in their large Harlem mansion.

Langley's hoarding began with collecting old newspapers and magazines in the 1930s. Over the years, the hoard grew to include a plethora of items such as old furniture, pianos, bicycles, cars, and a boat, resulting in the house being entirely cluttered with little space to move. Visitors had to maneuver through narrow paths between towering piles of objects.

In 1947, the police discovered Homer dead of starvation within the property. At the same time, Langley was found dead under a pile of debris. With over 100 tons of garbage needing removal, it took weeks to clear the mansion.

The Collyer Brothers' Hoard generated a considerable media buzz at the time and became an example of extreme hoarding. It prompted discussions on social isolation, mental health, and consumption. The house and its contents were auctioned off, and today, the Collyer brothers' story is a tragic reminder of unchecked hoarding and its dangers.

Some fascinating tidbits about the case include the mansion being described as a "maze of booby traps," as Langley had set up various obstacles to prevent intruders. The plethora of items removed displayed some value, including a painting by William Merritt Chase, sold for a hefty $24,000. After the house's clearance, the city demolished it, and today, the site is a park named after the Collyer brothers.

Through documentaries, books, and TV shows, the Collyer Brothers' story continues to captivate audiences. The hoard remains a cautionary tale, inspiring discussions on hoarding disorders and the broader cultural, social, and economic factors that drive hoarding behaviors.

The Dancing Mania of Strasbourg

The Dancing Mania of Strasbourg is a strange and fascinating event that took hold of the city's citizens in the summer of 1518. For several weeks, men and women danced uncontrollably in the streets, forming frenzied crowds that grew larger as more people joined in. This phenomenon had a profound impact on Strasbourg's social, religious, and medical spheres.

The city was a prosperous trading hub situated on the Rhine River during the Middle Ages, with a diverse population that included German, French, and Alsatian communities. However, Strasbourg experienced a series of crises and upheavals, including the Black Death, social unrest, and conflicts between the Catholic Church and the Protestant Reformation. These factors contributed to a sense of anxiety and uncertainty among the people, which may have played a role in the onset of the Dancing Mania.

The event began when a woman named Frau Troffea started to dance wildly in the street and was soon joined by dozens of others. The dancers were in an ecstatic state, sweating profusely, writhing on the ground, and sometimes even foaming at the mouth.

Authorities tried to contain the outbreak by setting up makeshift dance halls, but this plan failed, and the mania continued to spread. After about a month, the frenzy began to subside, leaving 50 to 400 people dead from exhaustion, heart attacks, or accidents.

The Dancing Mania had a lasting impact on Strasbourg's social and cultural landscape. It sparked medical and scientific debates about the causes of the mania, with some physicians attributing it to a collective mental illness or the effects of ergot poisoning. The event also inspired artistic and literary works, such as the famous woodcut by Hans Holbein the Younger.

Today, the Dancing Mania remains a mysterious and intriguing event that continues to capture the imagination of scholars and artists alike. It reminds us of the power of collective behaviour and the unexpected events that can shape our lives in unpredictable ways.

The mania was a complex and multi-faceted phenomenon that reflected the anxieties and tensions of its time. While there is no clear explanation for the Dancing Mania, historians agree that it was a significant event that had a profound impact on Strasbourg's social, religious, and medical spheres.

The Ourang Medan Mystery

In 1947, a Dutch cargo ship named the Ourang Medan was found adrift and abandoned in the Malacca Strait. The discovery of the vessel led to an extensive investigation that remains unsolved to this day. Built in 1919, the Ourang Medan transported goods for many years until it was seized by the Japanese as a transport ship during World War II. After the war, it was returned to Dutch ownership and once again operated as a commercial freighter. Its final voyage began when it left Sumatra, Indonesia, carrying a cargo of sulphur bound for the United States.

The distress signal from the Ourang Medan was received by the American vessel Silver Star, which immediately set out to find the stranded ship. The message indicated that all officers, including the captain, were dead and lying in the chartroom and bridge, with possibly the whole crew dead, too. When the Silver Star crew reached the Ourang Medan, they found no living people, only the corpses of the entire crew and a lifeless dog laying on the deck. There were no signs of injury, and even the ship's dog had its teeth bared, as if in a fight. While the Silver Star attempted to tow the abandoned ship to port, smoke started pouring out of the cargo hold, prompting the crew to abandon it before it exploded and sank.

The Ourang Medan mystery remains one of the most significant unsolved maritime disasters in history. Despite extensive investigations, no official explanation has been given for the events that took place on the ship. The incident has sparked numerous theories, including piracy, crew mutiny, and supernatural involvement. The story of the Ourang Medan has become part of maritime folklore and has been referenced in popular culture, including books, movies, and TV shows.

There are several interesting and lesser-known facts about the Ourang Medan mystery. The first written account of the incident appeared in a Dutch-Indonesian newspaper in 1948, a year after the events took place. Additionally, there are no official records of the Ourang Medan's existence before the incident, leading some to speculate that the ship never existed.

Despite all the theories and attempts to solve the mystery, the Ourang Medan remains an enigma that continues to capture the imagination of people around the world. The story is a fascinating one that has led to endless discussions about what could have happened on that ill-fated voyage. Volunteers have been searching for artifacts and answers for years, but so far, none have been found. Even though there is no definitive explanation for the incident, the story of the Ourang Medan remains an exciting mystery that fascinates and intrigues people to this day.

The 1955 Le Mans Disaster

The 1955 Le Mans Disaster is a heartbreaking event that occurred during the 23rd 24-hour race at the Circuit de la Sarthe in Le Mans, France. This tragic incident took place on June 11, 1955, and resulted in the deaths of 83 spectators and one driver, making it one of the deadliest motorsport accidents of all time.

At the time of the disaster, there was fierce competition among car manufacturers in Europe, and many countries were investing heavily in the development of new racing technologies. The Le Mans race was a highly anticipated event in the international racing calendar, attracting top teams and drivers from all over the world.

The accident took place when a Mercedes-Benz 300 SLR driven by Pierre Levegh crashed into the crowd after colliding with another car. The impact caused the car to disintegrate, with shrapnel flying into the crowd, resulting in multiple fatalities and injuries. The official death toll was 83, although sources suggest that the true number may have been higher.

This disaster raised concerns about safety standards in motorsport and led to a series of changes in regulations, including the introduction of safety barriers, improved vehicle design, and stricter controls on spectators.

The impact of the 1955 Le Mans Disaster was far-reaching, sparking a worldwide conversation about the dangers of motorsport and the need for greater safety measures. The accident forced teams and organizers to reassess their approach to racing, leading to a focus on driver and spectator safety that continues to this day. Families and loved ones of the victims still bear the scars of that devastating day.

It's worth noting that in response to this tragic event, Mercedes-Benz withdrew from racing for the next three decades, citing the Le Mans disaster as the reason. The disaster drew the critical attention of the world towards safety in motorsport, leading to sweeping reforms and innovations that continue to shape the sport today.

In modern times, the 1955 Le Mans Disaster is viewed as a turning point in motorsport history that marked a shift towards greater emphasis on safety and regulation. It's still a poignant reminder of the importance of safety measures at races. The event is also a warning against unchecked competition and the need for responsible racing practices. Tributes to the victims and reminders of the ongoing significance of safety measures are still observed at Le Mans.

The Zone of Silence

Deep in the heart of the rugged and desolate terrain of northern Mexico, lies a curious and otherworldly place known as the Zone of Silence. It is a patch of land where radio and communication signals cannot be transmitted, and it has been compared to the infamous Bermuda Triangle due to the strange and unexplained phenomena that occur there. The area is a mecca for UFO enthusiasts and conspiracy theorists who are drawn to the fascinating stories that surround it.

Located in the Mapimí Biosphere Reserve in the Chihuahuan Desert, the Zone of Silence is surrounded by rocky outcrops, sand dunes, and cactus populations. The region has a complex and tumultuous history, and it was once a hotbed of conflict between Mexican revolutionaries and the government. But it was an American missile test in 1970 that first drew attention to the area. The missile went off-course and fell into the Zone of Silence, which was largely unknown at the time. A team of American experts were sent in to retrieve the missile, but they found that radio signals were weak and GPS readings were erroneous. This was the beginning of a series of expeditions that would study the anomalous arena and report strange phenomena, including sightings of UFOs and the disappearance of aircraft.

Today, the Zone of Silence continues to be a magnet for those who are fascinated by the unexplained and paranormal. Many visitors claim to have experienced eerie and unexplained phenomena in the area, and scientists continue to study the Zone in an effort to understand its mysterious properties. However, the area remains shrouded in secrecy and debate, with no clear explanation for its anomalies.

Despite its mysterious reputation, the Zone of Silence has unique flora and fauna, including the Mapimí Silent Cricket, which is named after the area. Mexican scientists even discovered a new worm species in the Zone of Silence, which they named after the actress Audrey Hepburn.

While the Mexican government has made efforts in recent years to promote tourism in the area, the Zone of Silence remains an enigmatic location, shrouded in secrets and mystery. It continues to attract visitors from around the world who are interested in the paranormal and extraterrestrial life. The Zone of Silence is one of the many curiosities of our world that is still waiting to be fully explored and explained.

The Michigan Triangle

Exploring the Enigma of the Michigan Triangle
The Michigan Triangle, positioned in the Great Lakes region of North America, has gained notoriety over the years due to its strange events and unexplained disappearances. It is an area that covers the majority of Lake Michigan, with Manitowoc (Wisconsin), Ludington (Michigan), and Benton Harbor (Michigan) marking its three points.

Given the treacherous waters of Lake Michigan, it is not surprising that maritime disasters are not uncommon in the region. In fact, the area has seen hundreds of shipwrecks over the years. One of the earliest recorded instances of a shipwreck goes back to 1679 when the French ship, Le Griffon, sank in the waters of Lake Michigan. The unpredictable weather in the region has also caused several shipwrecks over time.

However, the Michigan Triangle has been the site of many inexplicable events. In the mid-twentieth century, the area was rocked by a series of strange happenings and eerie disappearances. One of the most well-known cases was the perplexing disappearance of the steamship Caribou on April 28, 1937. All 32 crew members on board vanished without a trace.

In 1950, two Michigan aircraft vanished within a week of each other while flying over Lake Michigan. Northwest Orient Airlines Flight 2501, carrying 58 passengers, and a military plane carrying 8 people, both disappeared under mysterious circumstances. Despite search efforts, no debris or bodies were ever found.

The Michigan Triangle has also been the source of other unexplained instances, including strange lights in the sky and unidentified flying objects. These incidents have led to speculation that the place may be haunted by supernatural and extraterrestrial forces. The Michigan Triangle has even been compared to the infamous Bermuda Triangle, another location renowned for bizarre disappearances. Some have suggested that the Michigan Triangle could be the lost city of Atlantis. However, others believe that natural factors like storms and underwater hazards are responsible for the disappearances.

The enigma surrounding the Michigan Triangle has fueled many debates and discussions, both in the scientific and paranormal communities. Safety regulations for ships and planes passing through the area have also increased due to the fascination with this unexplained territory. Despite decades of speculation, scientific inquiries, and a multitude of written works, the mystery of the Michigan Triangle remains unsolved.

The Wow! Signal

On a summer night in 1977, astronomer Jerry R. Ehman noted a strange signal on the printout of the Big Ear radio telescope at Ohio's University. The radio signal lasted for 72 seconds and was so strong that he couldn't ignore it. Ehman scribbled a single word in the margin - "Wow!".

The Big Ear radio telescope had been in operation for close to a decade, and it was among the powerful instruments used by NASA to search for extraterrestrial intelligence during the Voyager mission. The Wow! Signal was the most striking and mysterious thing it had discovered in all that time.

The signal was exceptionally strong, with a frequency of 1,420 MHz, the same as that of hydrogen. The most prevalent element in the universe. The signal hadn't been detected before and has not been detected since. Scientists tried to explain its origin, but every hypothesis they came up with defied the laws of physics.

The detection of the Wow! Signal sparked an insatiable interest in extraterrestrial life in the academic and scientific community. The event led to an increase in funding for research on the subject and prompted upgrades to the Big Ear radio telescope. The search for extraterrestrial intelligence became a priority for the scientific community.

It's fascinating to note that the signal was detected during the same year as the release of 'Close Encounters of the Third Kind.' Scientists have tried to replicate the signal, but their attempts have been unsuccessful. Despite the number of years that have gone by, the Wow! Signal remains an unexplained phenomenon, one of the most significant in history.

The Wow! Signal endures as it reignites our fascination and curiosity about the possibility of life beyond our planet. People all over the world remain captivated by the mysterious event, which still inspires endless discussions and theories.

The Great Blue Norther of 1911

The Great Blue Norther of 1911: A Lesson in the Power of Nature
During the early 1900s, the United States experienced a period of significant advancement in industry, technology, and communication. Despite these progressions, weather forecasting and monitoring tools were still in their developing stages, with limited resources available to predict sudden, extreme weather events. On November 11th, 1911, a cold front moved south from Canada and collided with a warm front over the central United States, resulting in a massive shift in temperature.

The country was swept with intense hurricane-force winds, thunderstorms, and heavy snowfall in some areas, with temperature drops reaching up to 60 degrees Fahrenheit. The sudden and unexpected weather change caught many people unprepared, resulting in widespread illness, accidents, and fatalities.

The Great Blue Norther of 1911 was an extraordinary event that occurred coincidentally with Armistice Day celebrations in many parts of the country. The temperature dropped from 76 degrees Fahrenheit to 11 degrees Fahrenheit in Kansas City, Missouri, and from 83 degrees Fahrenheit to 17 degrees Fahrenheit in Oklahoma City. The immediate aftermath of the Great Blue Norther included widespread disruption to transportation, communication, and agriculture.

Farmers lost their crops and livestock due to the sudden freeze, while trains and telegraph lines were severely affected by the stormy weather. The event highlighted the necessity of improved weather monitoring and forecasting, leading to the creation of more sophisticated tools and technologies in the years to come.

The Great Blue Norther of 1911 is a fascinating event in American history, demonstrating the raw power and unpredictable nature of our planet. The phrase "Great Blue Norther" was coined by Dallas Morning News reporter G.B. Metcalfe, who described it as "a great, blue, northern blizzard." The impact of the eruption of the Novarupta volcano in Alaska, which occurred earlier that year and may have changed weather patterns, is still debated.

This event serves as a reminder of the importance of being prepared for sudden weather changes, respecting the power of nature, and acknowledging the resilience and resourcefulness of communities in the face of adversity. While not as well-known as other weather events, such as hurricanes or tornadoes, the Great Blue Norther remains an awe-inspiring event that will undoubtedly remain a fascinating read in history books.

The Day The Music Died

The late 1950s saw a cultural revolution in the United States, with rock and roll music becoming increasingly popular. Buddy Holly, Ritchie Valens, and The Big Bopper were among the emerging artists who were dominating the charts at the time. Their music was exciting and fresh, and they took the world by storm in no time.

However, air travel wasn't as common then, and touring was the only way for them to reach a wider audience. Hence, they often relied on small planes, which weren't very reliable, safe, or equipped for flying in harsh weather conditions.

On February 3, 1959, tragedy struck when a small plane carrying Buddy Holly and his band, The Crickets, crashed in a cornfield in Clear Lake, Iowa, killing all four passengers on board, including the pilot. Among the passengers were Ritchie Valens and The Big Bopper, whose flu had convinced Waylon Jennings to give up his seat on the flight.

The impact of this tragedy was felt throughout the music industry, with fans and fellow musicians mourning the loss of three incredibly talented artists whose careers had been cut short. The incident marked a turning point for rock and roll in terms of safety and security when it came to touring.

Despite his untimely death, Buddy Holly's influence on rock and roll cannot be overstated. His innovative style paved the way for countless artists in the years following his death. The Beatles were among those inspired by his work and even took part of their name from Holly's band, The Crickets.

Tommy Allsup, who is famously known for losing a coin toss to Ritchie Valens for the final seat on the flight, went on to have a successful career as a guitarist and producer, working with artists such as Willie Nelson, Kenny Rogers, and Roy Orbison.

Even today, more than 60 years after the tragic plane crash, the legacy of these three rock and roll legends continues to inspire new generations of musicians. Their music remains popular, and their impact on the genre is undeniable. Although the world lost Buddy Holly, Ritchie Valens, and The Big Bopper on that fateful day in February 1959, their contribution to popular music will never be forgotten.

The Cleveland Torso Murders

The quiet streets of Cleveland, Ohio were shattered by a series of brutal murders between 1935 and 1938. At least twelve victims, mostly homeless or drifters, were discovered dismembered and decapitated, their remains left along the banks of the Cuyahoga River and in the nearby Kingsbury Run ravine. The killer was never identified, and his motives remain unknown, adding to the intrigue of this horrifying case that has never been solved.

The Great Depression and the end of Prohibition had hit the country hard, and Cleveland was struggling to cope with the challenges they presented. The Kingsbury Run area had earned itself a reputation as a seedy, lawless district, teeming with vice and crime. As the body count began to increase, the overburdened police force was unable to keep up with the investigation. Political corruption, poor evidence handling, and a lack of resources hampered the search for the killer.

Over the course of three years, the murderer's grisly handiwork became increasingly depraved. Victims, mostly men, were decapitated, dismembered, and sometimes posed in grotesque ways. The killer's barbarity was such that he removed the victims' teeth and fingers with the intention of remaining unidentified. Despite a massive manhunt and the involvement of the FBI, the killer was never caught, and the murders remain one of America's most infamous unsolved cases.

The impact of the Cleveland Torso Murders on the local community was significant. It exposed the inadequacies and corruption of law enforcement, leading to the creation of a civilian police review board. The murders also sparked public hysteria and conspiracy theories, with rumors of a "Mad Butcher of Kingsbury Run" who preyed on the city's most vulnerable.

The nature of the murders was particularly grisly, with hardly any blood at the crime scenes, no signs of sexual violence, and a confusing trail of clues. An unclaimed box of human remains was found in a train station, and a cryptic letter was sent to Eliot Ness, the famous federal agent. The murders were even speculated to have inspired the character of the "Torsotalker" in James Ellroy's novel, The Black Dahlia.

Decades later, the case continues to intrigue and fascinate the public. It has been the subject of multiple books, documentaries, and a graphic novel. In recent years, advances in DNA technology have led to renewed efforts to solve the case. The Cleveland Police Department has even exhumed the remains of several victims in hopes of bringing the killer to justice, but to no avail. The haunting legacy of the Cleveland Torso Murders speaks to our continued obsession with true crime and the chilling depths of human depravity.

The Pied Piper of Hamelin

Deep in the heart of Germany, amid the prosperous trading town of Hamelin, an extraordinary event took place in the 1300s. The legend of the Pied Piper, a tale of revenge and enchantment, has captivated audiences for centuries and continues to do so today.

In those times, Europe was engulfed in a devastating outbreak of the bubonic plague that took a toll on many towns and villages including Hamelin. The town was plagued by rats infesting every corner, and it is said that a magical piper was hired to rid the town of its vermin problem. The piper did as he was asked and led the rats out of the town, and into the River Weser where they met their end. But when it came time to pay the piper, the town refused his agreed-upon fee, and he took revenge by using his enchanting music to lure every child of the town to a fate unknown.

Some say that the children were led to a nearby cave and never seen again, while others claim that they were transported to a world of eternal happiness. The fate of the piper is shrouded in mystery, with some accounts suggesting that he met the same end as his rat companions.

The echoes of this tale have been heard over the centuries, retold in books, plays, and movies, and adapted in countless ways. Even in Hamelin itself, there is an annual festival celebrating the legend, with actors reenacting the tale and children dressing up in rat costumes, following the piper through the streets.

While the story may have some roots in historical fact, it is widely believed that it has been embellished over time to become the legend we know today. Yet the notion of stories that capture our imagination, that endure through time, continues to be as relevant now as it was in the 1300s when the Pied Piper first appeared. This tale is a testament to the power of storytelling that continues to captivate, inspire, and endure for generations.

The New England Dark Day

The year was 1780, and New England was deeply embroiled in the Revolutionary War. Times were tough, with crop failures and harsh weather conditions causing widespread hardship and struggle. But on May 19th, something truly extraordinary happened that would send fear and panic rippling through the region.

It started like any other day, with clear skies and bright sunshine. But as the day wore on, an eerie darkness descended, blotting out the sun and casting an otherworldly glow over the land. For hours, people huddled indoors, lighting candles and lamps in the middle of the day as the darkness refused to lift.

Some turned to religion, convinced that this was a sign of God's wrath. Others speculated wildly about the cause, ranging from wildfires to cosmic phenomena. And even after the darkness had finally dissipated, the strange event continued to haunt the region for years to come.

The New England Dark Day, as it came to be known, left a lasting impact on the people and the land. Crops suffered in the absence of sunlight, and daily life was disrupted as people struggled to cope with the strange and unsettling circumstances.

But despite its lasting legacy, the cause of the dark day remains shrouded in mystery. Was it the result of forest fires, as some have suggested? Or was there something more supernatural at play?

Even to this day, the New England Dark Day remains a symbol of the power of nature to confound and amaze us. It's a stark reminder of just how small we are in the face of the elements, and a testament to the resilience of the human spirit in the face of the unknown.

The Windsor Hum

The Windsor Hum, an unexplained phenomenon, has been plaguing residents of Windsor, Ontario, Canada, and surrounding areas since 2011. Though it has provoked countless theories, the hum remains shrouded in mystery and its cause unknown.

Situated near the US border and home to manufacturing plants and an abundance of noise pollution, Windsor offers a fertile environment for the hum to thrive. Despite this, experts have yet to pinpoint exactly what causes the strange, low-frequency rumble that sounds like a distant idling diesel engine and can be heard both indoors and out.

Many first complained about the hum in 2011, and it quickly drew media attention. Countless investigations and inquiries followed, though to date, none have yielded any answers. Some believe the hum may be tied to individual sensitivities or hearing damage, as in some cases, only certain people in households can hear it.

The hum has severely impacted the lives of those who hear it, causing sleep disturbances, headaches, and other health problems. It has even affected property values, with many hesitant to purchase a home in the area due to the ceaseless noise. The hum has gained attention from both the media and scientific community, with some residents attempting to capture the sound to prove their case.

The hum has extended far beyond Windsor, too; residents of Michigan, over 30 miles away, have reported hearing it. Yet despite the hum's continued prevalence, despite its impact on residents' lives and property values, and despite its widespread attention in both the media and scientific communities, the hum remains as mysterious and enigmatic as ever.

The Lake Michigan Triangle

Deep within Lake Michigan, between Manitowoc, Wisconsin, Ludington, and Benton Harbor, Michigan, lies the enigmatic Lake Michigan Triangle. This region has long been shrouded in mystery as it has been the site of numerous unexplained incidents over the years, making it one of the most peculiar and enigmatic places on the planet.

Sprawled within the United States, Lake Michigan is the third-largest of the Great Lakes, and its unique assemblage includes sand dunes, lighthouses, and contiguous forests that elevate its breathtaking landscape. However, the Lake Michigan Triangle adds an extra layer of thrill to the region, with its rumored supernatural phenomena.

The Lake Michigan Triangle has seen its fair share of bizarre events, from mysterious disappearances to shipwrecks and unexplained sightings. One of the most striking incidents dates back to April 28, 1937, when the steamship SS City of Milwaukee vanished within the Triangle's bounds with its 52 passengers. Nothing was ever found, including the wreckage, leading to several cases of reported unexplained disappearances, ghosts, sea monsters, and UFO sightings ever since.

The aftermath of these inexplicable incidents has had profound and distressing effects on both the families of the victims and the locals. However, the Triangle's mystique has also led to increased tourism while arousing fear and unease among residents. Despite ongoing research and theoretical attempts to explain these events, the Lake Michigan Triangle remains an unsolved mystery.

The Triangle is said to be responsible for over 40 ship and plane vanishing acts, with no definite source of explanation available so far. Reports even suggest that the region is home to countless time warps, portals, and paranormal activity. One of the craziest tales involves a sailor who claimed he had been transported from the early 1800s to 1982 after accidentally traveling through dense fog in the area.

Today, the Lake Michigan Triangle is an increasingly popular destination for adventurous travelers seeking to unmask its supernatural secrets. It's a place that inspires awe and fear, and for good reason. The enigmatic region remains an intriguing enigma, holding on to its veil of mystery with several unanswered questions.

The Curse of the Pharaohs

Unearthing the Mysterious Curse of the Pharaohs: A Tale from Ancient Egypt

Egypt has always been a land of intrigue and fascination, steeped in history, myths, and legends. For centuries, the people of Egypt have held the belief that curses can bring misfortune, illness, and death to those who violate the resting places of their ancestors.

In the early 20th century, archaeologist Howard Carter uncovered the long-lost tomb of King Tutankhamun, which had been sealed for over 3,000 years. The discovery of the tomb was a momentous occasion and thrilled people worldwide. However, the Egyptians were deeply disturbed by this violation, fearing that it would trigger the Curse of the Pharaohs, a terrible event that had haunted their history.

The Curse of the Pharaohs was said to be a curse placed on tomb violators, which brought about inexplicable and tragic deaths. According to legend, it was believed that King Tutankhamun's tomb was cursed, and those who disturbed its peace would suffer a terrible fate.

On November 26, 1922, Howard Carter and his team successfully opened the tomb's sealed door, revealing a treasure trove of ancient artifacts. However, the excitement was short-lived, as tragedy quickly followed.

The first victim of the supposed curse was Lord Carnarvon, who was the financial backer of the mission, and died only months after the tomb's opening. His death was attributed to a mosquito bite that led to a bacterial infection, but others believed that it was the curse of the pharaohs that led to his demise.

Over the following years, several other members of the expedition died under strange circumstances linked to the curse, including the financier who funded the mission and the head of the Egyptian Antiquities Board. These incidents were highly publicized, and the curse theory gained popularity.

The Curse of the Pharaohs had a significant impact on Egyptology and popular culture at the time. It sparked renewed interest in the ancient mysteries of Egypt and heightened respect for the Egyptians and their ancestral beliefs concerning the safekeeping of Pharaohs' tombs.

However, the curse also instilled a sense of fear and suspicion among people associated with the discovery of King Tutankhamun's tomb. It also perpetuated negative stereotypes and biases regarding Egypt and the Egyptians as many believed that the curse was evidence of their superstitious and exotic culture.

The Stone-Throwing Devil of New Castle

In the quaint and peaceful colonial town of New Castle, Delaware, a bizarre and unsettling event occurred in the mid-18th century. The townspeople were plagued by an unseen force responsible for hurling stones through the air. Many attributed this occurrence to the work of the devil, and mass hysteria ensued. This phenomenon became known as the Stone-Throwing Devil of New Castle, and has since remained one of the most enigmatic and perplexing events in colonial American history.

New Castle was founded by the Dutch in the mid-17th century and occupied by the British. The town was a prosperous and religious community, highly superstitious in nature. With supernatural beliefs and a history of strange occurrences, such as outbreaks of smallpox and yellow fever, it was not a far stretch for the townspeople to attribute the occurrences to the devil.

In April 1728, a group of children playing in the town square witnessed stones seemingly arise out of nowhere, hitting one of them in the head. These stones rained down, and people saw that they were coming from above, flying over rooftops and even defying gravity. Witnesses reported seeing a dark figure flying alongside the stones, whom they believed to be the Devil himself.

The strange happenings continued for several months, with rocks being thrown at buildings, people, and even inside homes. The town was terrified, and many believed the devil was responsible, possibly due to New Castle's supposed sinful ways. Some accused witches of being behind the events, resulting in a witch hunt. This led to innocent individuals being accused of witchcraft and even caused one local Quaker, Moll Dyer, to flee the town and be later found dead in the woods.

Despite attempts to explain the phenomenon, no rational explanation was given. The stone-throwing devil eventually ceased its activity as mysteriously as it began. The incident had a profound effect on New Castle, leading to widespread fear, a damaged reputation, and persecution of innocent individuals.

Although largely forgotten today, the Stone-Throwing Devil of New Castle remains an eerie and mysterious event in American history. Some believe the occurrence to be evidence of demonic activity, while skeptics see it as a case of mass hysteria. Whatever the cause, this event is a powerful reminder of the fear of the unknown and the dangerous power of superstition.

The War of the Worlds Broadcast

On a cool fall evening in 1938, millions of Americans tuned in to their radio sets to listen to the popular CBS radio drama show, The Mercury Theatre on the Air. What ensued would go down in history as one of the most infamous broadcasts of all-time, known as "The War of the Worlds Broadcast." This fictional tale of an alien invasion of Earth caused widespread fear and panic amongst listeners, sparking conversations about the power of media and the blurry line between fact and fiction.

The 1930s were a time of great uncertainty for Americans, as the country emerged from the Great Depression, while tensions mounted with Nazi Germany. Radio was a popular entertainment form, offering immediate access to news and drama programming. Orson Welles, a rising star in theatre, film, and radio, produced his dramatic adaptation of H.G. Wells' classic novel, The War of the Worlds, in this context.

As Halloween approached in 1938, The Mercury Theatre on the Air aired a modern retelling of The War of the Worlds. Orson Welles provided an introduction, explaining that the upcoming program was a work of fiction. However, many listeners missed the disclaimer and believed the broadcast to be genuine news. The show presented a news-style broadcast detailing a series of strange events happening in different parts of the country, ending with a reporter describing the chaotic invasion of aliens.

The show was so well-produced that it induced mass panic across the country, with people fleeing their homes and calling the police. The aftermath of the broadcast caused a media firestorm, attracting both praise and criticism from audiences. The event had a lasting impact on American culture and media, sparking debates about broadcast media's responsibility to provide accurate information.

The incident resulted in the FCC mandating regulations that required broadcasters to be more explicit and transparent in their disclaimers. The War of the Worlds Broadcast holds a prominent place in both media and radio history as a cautionary tale, and the power of storytelling and sound effects.

The Apollo 13 Mission

In 1970, the Apollo 13 mission launched into space with the aim of landing on the moon and collecting samples. This ambitious undertaking was fraught with danger, and the lives of the three astronauts on board soon hung in the balance. An unexpected explosion on the spacecraft caused a near-fatal crisis that called upon the bravery and ingenuity of everyone involved.

The Apollo 13 was launched amidst the intense competition between the United States and the Soviet Union known as the Space Race. The astronauts had to go through rigorous training to ensure they were ready for the challenges of space travel. The mission was risky and complex, but the United States had already achieved success with the Apollo 11 landing on the moon.

Two days into the mission, a malfunction in one of the oxygen tanks caused an explosion that damaged the spacecraft and put the astronauts' lives in danger. The crew quickly assessed the damage and radioed back to Earth the famous phrase, "Houston, we have a problem." The crew was stranded with a loss of electrical power, water, and propulsion, hundreds of thousands of miles away from Earth.

Ground support teams of NASA engineers worked tirelessly to bring the astronauts back home, improvising solutions for a multitude of technical problems. Improvements were made to spaceship designs and space suits to improve their safety. Nevertheless, the astronauts still had to ration their remaining resources, such as food and water, until they could return home.

Despite the challenging circumstances, all three astronauts returned safely to Earth, thanks to the incredible bravery and resourcefulness of the crew and ground support staff. It was a feat that inspired the entire country. NASA learned numerous lessons from the Apollo 13 mission, making space travel and technology safer.

The Apollo 13 mission has become a fascinating subject for popular culture references, books, and documentaries. It is still viewed as one of the most remarkable achievements in human history. The bravery and ingenuity demonstrated during the crisis, even when human lives were at stake, remain relevant today. It continues to inspire people to explore the unknown, to push beyond known boundaries, and to always be prepared for the unexpected.

The New Madrid Earthquake

The New Madrid Earthquake of 1811-1812 was one of the most powerful seismic events in US history, with its epicenter located in the town of New Madrid, Missouri. At the time of the earthquake, the area was still being explored and settled, with Native American tribes, French fur traders, and Spanish explorers having all passed through the region.

Known for its seismic activity, the area was rocked by four major quakes and over 2,000 smaller aftershocks, causing the Mississippi River to reverse its flow and creating enormous fissures that swallowed entire trees. The earthquake was so intense that its impact was felt as far away as New York City, Boston, and Montreal.

John James Audubon, who was living in Kentucky at the time of the earthquake, was able to observe its effects on the natural world nearby. One of the most notable consequences of the earthquake was the creation of a new island, Reelfoot Lake, now located in Tennessee.

In the aftermath of the New Madrid Earthquake, the sparsely populated area around New Madrid suffered significant damage. Many homes and buildings were destroyed, and the earthquake is believed to have been responsible for a widespread outbreak of influenza in the region. However, the event ultimately contributed to a deeper understanding of seismic activity and its impact on the natural world.

The earthquake continues to be studied by geologists and seismologists as an example of how large earthquakes can impact areas with low population densities. Though it is not as well-known as more recent natural disasters like Hurricane Katrina or the 1906 San Francisco earthquake, the New Madrid Earthquake remains a significant event in American history.

Some fascinating facts include that the earthquake was so powerful it destroyed the town of New Madrid and even rang church bells as far away as Boston. Reports suggest that small earthquakes are still occurring in the region today, continuing to remind us of the power of nature.

The Chicago Tylenol Murders

In September 1982, the Chicago Tylenol Murders made headlines across the country. What started as a typical day for many Chicagoans soon turned deadly after seven people died mysteriously from consuming cyanide-laced Tylenol capsules. This event quickly became one of the most notorious and unsolved cases in American history.

At the time of the murders, Tylenol was a leading over-the-counter pain medication. The Chicago area was in the midst of a pharmaceutical revolution, and consumers were becoming more health-conscious, turning to OTC drugs instead of visiting doctors. This change in lifestyle led to a surge in the sale of Tylenol.

Over a period of three days, seven people died after taking Tylenol. Authorities discovered that the capsules had been tampered with, and the poison had been inserted into bottles in grocery stores and pharmacies. Despite a manhunt, the killer was never found.

The Tylenol murders led to significant changes in the packaging of consumer goods. Tamper-proof packaging was introduced, where the safety seal cannot be broken without destruction, and this was widely adopted across the food and drug industry. The crisis also impacted public trust in the industry, with extra safety measures put in place.

The FBI conducted its largest investigation, involving over 1200 individuals, in the aftermath of the Tylenol murders. The original manufacturer, Johnson & Johnson, issued a nationwide recall, destroying over 31 million Tylenol capsules at a cost of $100 million. The case remains unsolved and is still considered one of the greatest crime puzzles of all time.

The Tylenol murders continue to be a cautionary tale, reminding people of the devastating power of a single act of tampering. The event is still remembered as a critical turning point in the way people consume over-the-counter drugs. From a corporate perspective, Johnson & Johnson took swift action to recall the drug and introduce tamper proof packaging to prevent similar incidents in the future. The legacy of the Tylenol murders lives on as a reminder to remain vigilant in all aspects of healthcare.

The Jonestown Massacre

On November 18, 1978, a tragedy unfolded in a remote settlement called Jonestown, South America, that would shock and haunt the world for years after. It was orchestrated by Jim Jones, the charismatic yet enigmatic leader of the Peoples Temple - a church he had formed in the 1950s in Indianapolis, Indiana. With a message of racial equality and social justice, the People's Temple quickly grew in popularity, attracting mostly working-class and minority members. However, as time wore on, Jones's behavior became increasingly erratic, leading to concerns among his followers. In the end, it was their worst fears that were realized.

In 1974, after highly publicized confrontations with local authorities, Jones moved the Peoples Temple to Guyana to establish Jonestown as a communal settlement. By 1978, reports of abuse and human right violations had reached a fever pitch, and a delegation of U.S. lawmakers arrived to investigate. But Jones, paranoid and convinced that the U.S. government was plotting against him, had other plans. He ordered his followers to prepare for a "revolutionary suicide" - a mass suicide to protest against the supposed cruelty of capitalism and to protect their way of life.

During the hours that followed, Jones dictated a manifesto, played recordings of speeches by prominent leaders, and announced the need for a "mass suicide." Some complied willingly, while others were forced at gunpoint or through injections. Children too young to understand what was happening were killed first, followed by their mothers and fathers. The results were catastrophic, with over 900 people, including women, men, and children, perishing in the tragic event, now known as the Jonestown Massacre.

The impact of the Jonestown Massacre was far-reaching, with people across the globe left stunned by the high number of young children who were victims of the cult. It brought attention to the dangerous, psychologically manipulative practices of cult leaders and led to tighter regulations on religious organizations. The events also caused widespread criticism of U.S. intelligence-gathering activities, which had been monitoring Jones's activities for some time.

The legacy of Jonestown serves as a cautionary tale and a reminder of how dangerous charismatic leaders can be. Survivor Odell Rhodes, who was in Jonestown the day of the massacre, has since dedicated his life to helping others who have left or escaped from cults. Fittingly, the Jonestown Massacre continues to be used as a case study to educate the public about the essential nature of being aware of the manipulation tactics of cult leaders and the need to remain vigilant to protect one's mental and emotional wellbeing.

The Mysterious Death of Edgar Allan Poe

Edgar Allan Poe, one of America's most renowned authors, poet, and literary critic, died under mysterious circumstances on October 7, 1849, sending shockwaves across the literary world. He was known for his dark and enigmatic writings, often exploring the supernatural, horror, and death in his works.

During his lifetime, he was grappling with several personal and professional setbacks such as financial difficulties, alcoholism, and an emotionally draining romantic life. In search of better career prospects, Poe traveled to Baltimore where he went missing while on his way to meet his fiancé, only to be found a few days later, delirious and disoriented, on the streets wearing clothes that did not belong to him.

He was taken to a hospital where he died four days later, at the age of 40, incoherent and unable to explain the events leading up to his disappearance.

The cause of his death remains a mystery to this day with several theories and speculations surrounding his death, ranging from medical conditions such as brain lesions, epilepsy, and alcohol poisoning to foul play such as murder and even suicide.

The death of Edgar Allan Poe has had a profound impact on American literature and culture. His work had already gained popularity during his lifetime, but his enigmatic death contributed to his legacy as a tortured artist with renewed interest in his life and work.

His grave site in Baltimore has become a tourist attraction, with visitors leaving items such as coins, pens and roses on his grave, while theories about his death range from alcohol poisoning and tuberculosis to rabies, and even murder by cooping.

Today, the mysterious circumstances leading up to Poe's death continues to intrigue audiences worldwide, keeping alive his legacy as one of the greatest writers of his generation. Though his personal life and contributions to American literature are repeatedly scrutinized and debated, no one can deny the lasting impact he has had on both American and international literature.

The Donner Party

The Donner Party – a name that invokes shivers down the spine of anyone familiar with the horrors of American history. This was a group of families who dared to embark on the treacherous journey from Illinois to California in 1846, brimming with hope and opportunism.

The early 19th century was marked by Manifest Destiny, a notion that propagated the idea of American expansionism across North America. With the hopes of finding new land, resources, and opportunities, pioneers and settlers moved westward. This journey was beset with danger; many faced disease, attacks, or harsh conditions – often disappearing, or succumbing to the unforgiving wilderness.

The Donner Party, led by George Donner, was a group of 87 people, comprising families, women, children, and a few single men, who decided to take a shortcut through the Sierra Nevada mountains in October 1846.

As fate would have it, a snowstorm began that lasted several months, leaving the group trapped, and struggling for survival. With inadequate supplies, clothing, and shelter, the group resorted to eating their pack animals and even boiled hides to survive. When the food eventually ran out, they were forced to resort to the unthinkable – cannibalism. In the end, of the 87 members, only 47 survived.

The impact of this catastrophic journey was profound, leading to increased emphasis on preparation, planning, and caution for westward expansion. The incident made the Oregon-California trail a matter of national importance and led to significant improvements of the route and infrastructure.

The Donner Party continues to captivate the public imagination, representing the darker aspects of American history, and a stark reminder of the harsh realities of westward expansion.

The story has been retold in books, films, and TV shows, depicting the desperation of the pioneers and the gruesome details of their cannibalistic acts. Nevertheless, the Donner Party remains a historically significant event, a testament to the indomitable nature of the American spirit, and the human will to survive in the face of unimaginable hardship.

The Great Thunderstorm of Widecombe-in-the-Moor

The Great Thunderstorm of Widecombe-in-the-Moor is a haunting and mysterious event that occurred on October 21, 1638. The village, situated in the Dartmoor National Park in England, was struck by a raging storm that caused destruction, injury, and death.

But what made this thunderstorm so unusual was the eerie and bizarre phenomena that accompanied it, which had never been seen before. Villagers reported hearing strange noises, seeing ghostly apparitions, and feeling an unusual chill in the air.

At the time, England was in the midst of the English Civil War, and many people attributed the thunderstorm to divine retribution or a sign of impending doom. The storm destroyed the church of St. Pancras, killing the vicar and several parishioners, and it left lasting scars on the landscape, including the split boulder known as "the Widecombe Thunderstone."

The Great Thunderstorm of Widecombe-in-the-Moor had a profound impact on the local community and wider society, challenging the prevailing beliefs of the time about natural disasters, God's role in human affairs, and the limits of human knowledge. Scholars debated whether the storm was caused by a rare meteorological phenomenon or a manifestation of the occult or paranormal.

Today, the thunderstorm is still remembered and celebrated in the area, with guided tours, museums, and festivals dedicated to its history and significance. It continues to inspire wonder and curiosity in people of all ages, reminding us of the awe-inspiring power of nature.

The Mysterious Life and Death of Kaspar Hauser

The Intriguing Tale of Kaspar Hauser

In 1828, a peculiar man named Kaspar Hauser appeared in Nuremberg, Germany, leaving those who encountered him baffled and bewildered. He was unable to communicate and had trouble standing upright. Hauser claimed that he had lived in a dark cell for most of his life, with minimal access to the outside world and little food and water.

His captor only taught him to read and write through indirect methods and remained mostly silent. His sudden arrival in Germany made him a sensation among politicians and scientists, but not everyone welcomed him.

Hauser's traumatic upbringing led to several physical and mental health issues that he struggled with. In 1833, he was stabbed in a park and died several days later. Despite the passage of time, the truth about his identity and experience remains a mystery, inspiring artistic, literary, and musical works.

Numerous theories exist regarding the circumstances of Kaspar Hauser's life, but none have been proven. He may have been a prince who was kidnapped or the illegitimate son of a noble family. Alternatively, he may have been raised in isolation as part of a social experiment or commentary.

Hauser's tale has left a significant impact on society and culture, inspiring adaptations into books, films, and plays. Researchers and scholars continue to investigate his mysterious case to uncover more clues about his baffling existence.

More than a century has passed since Hauser arrived in Nuremberg and his subsequent death, but his story remains a fascinating and intriguing mystery. The lack of concrete evidence surrounding his identity and experience has only added to the allure of his tale, with many people around the world drawn to the enigma surrounding him. Some have even suggested that his story may have inspired the character of Frankenstein's monster.

Kaspar Hauser's legacy has continued to live on through various works of art, literature, and cultural references. His story raises profound questions about human nature and experience, such as the consequences of being raised in isolation and the impact of basic human interaction and companionship. These are complex issues that continue to fascinate and challenge us today, making Kaspar Hauser's story one that will likely continue to captivate the imagination of people from all walks of life for years to come.

The Pollock Twins: A Case of Possible Reincarnation

The story of The Pollock Twins is nothing less than a spectacle. It all began in post-World War II England, where John and Florence Pollock welcomed two daughters, Joanna and Jacqueline, into their family. Tragically, both girls passed away in a car accident at the tender ages of six and 11, devastating their parents.

But, things took a bizarre turn when John and Florence proclaimed a few years later that their new daughters, Gillian and Jennifer, were the reincarnations of Joanna and Jacqueline. The family's ensuing story, which became known as 'The Pollock Twins: A Case of Possible Reincarnation,' has left people flabbergasted and mystified ever since.

To give some background, the idea of reincarnation is deeply rooted in ancient cultures, including Indian and Greek civilizations. However, post-war England was certainly not a hotbed for this concept. Hence, when John and Florence claimed that their daughters were the reincarnations of their deceased children, many dismissed it as a fantasy — that is, until they witnessed the strange behavior of their new daughters.

Gillian and Jennifer were uncannily reminiscent of Joanna and Jacqueline in how they conducted themselves. For instance, Gillian possessed a noticeable birthmark just like Joanna, and Jennifer's birthmark mimicked Jacqueline's. Additionally, Jennifer had a proclivity for toy cars and dolls- a quality of Jacqueline's when she was alive. Similarly, Gillian shared Jacqueline's fear of water bodies.

The strangest element in this saga involves the girls recalling events, some of which had occurred before they were born. For instance, Gillian accurately regaled details about a house and the garden her deceased sister had described to her earlier. Even more eerily, Gillian remembered the name of the nurse who had taken care of her in her past life- detailing a wart on the nurse's hand. To their parents' amazement, the nurse did have a wart on her hand!

The whole conundrum surrounding The Pollock Twins' case continues to divide people to this day, resulting in a raging debate. While some still brush it aside as a mere coincidence, believers firmly assert the opposite. Regardless of the perspective, one can glean ample fascination from the story. The tale has even been turned into a movie, perhaps testifying to the pull it has on people's imagination.

The 1908 New York to Paris Car Race

The 1908 New York to Paris Car Race: A Historic Moment for the Automobile Industry

The 1908 New York to Paris Car Race is widely regarded as one of the most significant moments in the history of the automobile industry. Initiated by the French newspaper "Le Matin" in 1907, the race was designed to showcase the capabilities of the innovative creations that were rapidly transforming transportation. The event was also meant to demonstrate that automobiles were reliable and could travel vast distances without breaking down.

At the time, the world was still struggling to develop reliable, high-performance automobiles. Long-distance journeys were rare, and the infrastructure to support such ventures was inadequate. The New York to Paris Car Race was a demonstration of the potential of the automobile industry, with a route that traversed unforgiving terrain, desert regions, and mountain ranges, making it one of the most challenging events of the time.

On February 12, 1908, six competing teams set out on the arduous journey, including three American teams, two from Europe, and one from Italy. The teams traveled from New York to San Francisco before crossing the Pacific Ocean and continuing through Alaska, Siberia, Russia, and Germany, before finally arriving in Paris. The route was perilous, with competitors facing harsh weather conditions, deep mud, and mechanical failures.

After overcoming numerous challenges, the American team of George Schuster, Montague Roberts, and George Miller emerged victorious, driving a Thomas Flyer. The triumph of the team marked the first occasion that the journey had been completed. The race inspired the need for better regulation of the industry and better roads to support longer journeys.

The event produced numerous fascinating anecdotes, such as the modified Thomas Flyer with a collapsible top used for repairs during the race. In Russia, competitors resorted to covering substantial distances using railway tracks since the roads were impassable, adding a whole new level of difficulty to the race. Furthermore, the Italian team became lost in the Siberian wilderness and was rescued by a group of hunters who guided them to the nearest village.

The 1908 New York to Paris Car Race remains a seminal moment in car racing and the history of transportation. It continues to captivate automotive enthusiasts and historians alike, inspiring modern-day rallies and races. The event demonstrated the remarkable spirit and determination of early adventurers who dared to traverse such a challenging and momentous journey.

The Bennington Triangle Disappearances

In the remote corner of southwestern Vermont lies the Bennington Triangle, a region steeped in folklore, witchcraft, and supernatural mysteries. This area boasts tales of forbidden love, ghostly apparitions, and inexplicable occurrences. But the most chilling of these stories is that of the Bennington Triangle Disappearances that occurred between 1945 and 1950, leaving a trail of confusion and fear in its wake.

It all began when a 74-year-old hunter, Middie Rivers, vanished without a trace in November 1945. Only two weeks later, 18-year-old Paula Welden went on a hike and was never seen again. The area surrounding Glastenbury Mountain was heavily wooded and sparsely populated, making it difficult to find any sign of the missing individuals. Over the next few years, two more people disappeared, including an eight-year-old boy and a veteran who had gone camping with his family.

Despite massive search efforts involving hundreds of people, no clues to the whereabouts of the missing individuals were ever found. Numerous strange occurrences and sightings occurred in the area during this time, including mysterious lights in the sky, ghostly voices, and reports of a haunting figure seen before some of the disappearances.

The Bennington Triangle Disappearances caused hysteria and disbelief in the local communities, with many people avoiding the area altogether. Some believed that the mountains were cursed or haunted, while others thought that a serial killer was on the loose. The case gained national attention and led to calls for stricter search and rescue protocols.

One of the most peculiar aspects of the case was the vanishing of James E. Tetford, a resident of the Bennington Soldier's Home. Tetford was traveling on a bus through the region when he disappeared without a trace during the journey. Strangely, his belongings were found on the bus, and some passengers recall seeing him sitting in his seat one moment and vanishing in the next.

To this day, the Bennington Triangle Disappearances remain an unsolved mystery, sparking a flurry of theories and speculations that range from the supernatural to Bigfoot and alien sightings. Yet, the Bennington Triangle continues to leave an indelible mark on the minds of people, serving as a chilling reminder of the dangers that lurk in the realm of the unknown.

The Sinking of the Wilhelm Gustloff

Remembering the Tragic Sinking of the Wilhelm Gustloff during World War II
The German cruise liner, Wilhelm Gustloff, was on a mission to evacuate as
many lives as possible during the final days of World War II. However, on
January 30th, 1945, tragedy struck when a Soviet submarine, S-13, fired four
torpedoes at the ship, causing it to sink in the frozen Baltic Sea. The disaster
claimed over 9,400 lives, primarily of women, children, and wounded soldiers,
marking it as the deadliest maritime disaster in history.

As chaos ensued within an hour of the ship sinking, passengers desperately
attempted to escape the approaching Soviet Army, with many jumping into
the freezing waters in the hope of reaching nearby ships. However, the
majority of passengers were trapped in the ship's cabins, unable to escape.

While overshadowed by larger atrocities in the years following the war, the
sinking of the Wilhelm Gustloff has recently been revisited in books, films, and
documentaries, bringing attention to the tragedy's impact on the war. The ship
was named after a prominent Nazi martyr, Gustav Wilhelm Stresemann, and
was originally built for Nazi propaganda purposes, serving as a reminder of the
ruthless nature of propaganda.

The tragedy's significance is evident in its mention in Albert Speer's memoirs
and use as evidence at the Nuremberg trials. Today, the Wilhelm Gustloff
disaster remains a tragic event, reminding us of the innocent lives lost during
the tumultuous period of World War II.

In recent years, efforts have been made to remember and honor the victims of
the Wilhelm Gustloff disaster. Every year on January 30th, a memorial service
is held in the town of Neustadt, where many of the survivors were brought
after the sinking. Additionally, there are several museums and monuments
dedicated to the tragedy, providing an opportunity for people to learn about
the event and pay their respects.

The sinking of the Wilhelm Gustloff serves as a reminder of the devastating
impact of war on innocent civilians. It is a tragic event that should never be
forgotten, and one that highlights the importance of peace, understanding,
and compassion. By remembering the victims and their stories, we can work
towards a better future, free from the horrors of war and violence.

The Hinterkaifeck Murders

In a small Bavarian village in 1922, an unimaginable crime shook the community to its core. The Hinterkaifeck Murders involved the gruesome killing of six members of the Gruber family, who resided on a secluded farm. Even after almost a century, the case still baffles many and remains one of the most enigmatic true crime events in history.

Germany was reeling from the aftermath of World War I, a time of political turmoil and instability, when the murders occurred. The Gruber family dwelling was in a tightly-knit community known for its conservatism and distrust of outsiders, making it all the more perplexing how such a tragic event could happen unnoticed.

On the night of March 31, 1922, the entire Gruber family was brutally murdered inside their home. Their bodies were discovered days later by a neighbor who became worried after not seeing them for some time. Andreas Gruber, the head of the family, his wife, daughter, daughter's two children, and a maid were all victims of the attack. Evidence shows that they had been lured to the barn, where they were struck with a mattock tool.

Despite thorough investigations, the case remains unsolved and the killer has yet to be identified. There have been numerous theories about the motive, ranging from a family feud to an unsettled romance, or even the involvement of supernatural forces.

The Hinterkaifeck Murders had far-reaching effects on German society. The crime left people shocked and frightened, forcing law enforcement to enhance their investigation techniques and develop new forensic methods to solve intricate cases like this one.

Several eerie details add to the mystique of the case. For instance, there is evidence that suggests the killer stayed at the farm for some days after the murders, looking after the animals and completing some tasks. This is an eerie thought that has led many to question the possible motives of the killer.

There has been speculation that the perpetrator may have been a soldier suffering from PTSD, which was very poorly understood and treated at the time. While this theory has yet to be proven, it highlights the unexpected ways in which the aftermath of the war affected individuals and society.

The Hinterkaifeck Murders remain a captivating subject for historians and true crime enthusiasts. The unsolved case has been the subject of various movies, books, and TV shows, and the chilling event continues to intrigue and mystify people across the world.

The Lady of the Dunes

Have you ever heard of the Lady of the Dunes? It's a disturbingly intriguing story about a gruesome murder that occurred in Provincetown, Massachusetts back in 1974. The victim, who remained unknown for over 20 years, was finally identified as "Mary Lee Bocchicchio" in 2010. Unfortunately, despite multiple leads and extensive investigation, the killer remains unknown to this day.

Provincetown, located at the tip of Cape Cod, was a popular tourist destination known for its picturesque beaches and colorful LGBT community. The 1970s was a period of significant social change, and Provincetown was no exception. The hippie culture was thriving, creating an artistic haven that sparked an area known for partying and drug use where the Lady of the Dunes' body was found.

One fateful day in July, a young girl walking her dog stumbled upon a partially decomposed body buried in the sand. The victim was a woman aged between 25 and 49, identified solely by her unshaven pubic hair, and had been strangled with a pair of blue jeans. She was also found with a blue bandana tied around her neck and a gold fleur-de-Lis earring. Despite extensive investigation, her identity remained a mystery for over two decades.

As a result of this heinous crime, the Lady of the Dunes' case was featured in Stephen King's novel "Joyland," which sparked renewed interest in the early 2000s. There are many rumors surrounding the Lady of the Dunes case, including a possible connection to the film "Jaws," which was shot in the area.

A woman that bore a striking resemblance to the Lady of the Dunes was spotted in the background of a beach scene. There was also a claim by a man known as the "Mad Bomber of New York" that he had some information about the murder, but it was never corroborated.

The Lady of the Dunes is one of the most intriguing unsolved cases in American history. Despite various podcasts, documentaries, and articles, the lack of information and the killer's identity contributes to its continued fascination. It remains a chilling reminder that some mysteries remain unsolved, and the truth may never be fully known.

The Patomskiy Crater Mystery

Deep in the Siberian Taiga, close to the border of Mongolia and Russia, lies a geological marvel that has left scientists and conspiracy theorists alike stumped for nearly a century now. The Patomskiy Crater, first discovered in 1949, measures approximately 160 meters deep and 500 meters wide, and stands out as an anomaly in the vast, wild landscape of the region.

But the mystery surrounding the Patomskiy Crater doesn't stop there. The surrounding area has a long history of unusual and unexplained occurrences - from harsh weather conditions and unique species of animals and plants to stories of shamans and mystical beings, the Siberian Taiga has always been shrouded in mystery. Legends and ancient myths tell of spirits that guard the secrets of the land and the people who live there, adding an eerie and mysterious atmosphere to the already-compelling Patomskiy Crater.

It was Soviet geologist Vadim Kolpakov who first stumbled across the Patomskiy Crater 72 years ago, calling for further investigation into its origins due to its unique, flat-bottomed bowl shape. Despite multiple scientific teams investigating the area since then, the exact cause of the crater remains a mystery to this day.

Theories abound - some scientists think that it could be a result of volcanic or tectonic activity, while others suggest that it may be a sinkhole caused by the gradual erosion of the surrounding landscape- but none have been accepted by the scientific community as a whole.

Despite the lack of a conclusive explanation, the Patomskiy Crater has had a significant impact on both science and society. Ongoing research into the area has captured the imaginations of people around the world, resulting in increased tourism and exploration. The mystery surrounding the crater has even pushed scientists to reconsider their theories about geology, landscape formation, and extraterrestrial activity.

It's not just the lack of explanation that makes the Patomskiy Crater so fascinating, however - there are also a few fun facts that add to its allure. For example, the crater was named after the nearby Patom River, and originally, its depth was estimated to be 100 meters before being revised to 160 meters. In the center of the crater is a small lake, with a depth of 67 meters, and local legends suggest that the crater was created by a god or spirit to mark the spot where they emerged from the earth.

Today, the Patomskiy Crater remains an attraction for those interested in Siberian folklore and nature, as well as scientists looking to solve the mystery of its creation.

The Nazca Lines

In the Nazca desert of southern Peru, an incredible mystery resides. The Nazca Lines are a series of massive geoglyphs that can only be seen in their entirety from high in the air. These mysterious etchings depict animals, geometric shapes, and humanoid figures that boggle the mind and inspire intrigue as to how they were created. The Nazca culture thrived in the area between 200 BCE and 600 CE and left behind this awe-inspiring creation.

The Nazca people were a pre-Columbian civilization known for their skilled pottery making and weaving. They also developed exceptional irrigation and water management systems. Their religious beliefs centered on the natural world, and they viewed everything as having a spirit. The Nazca Lines were created as a form of religious expression, particularly as an offering to the gods believed to live in the sky.

The geoglyphs were made by removing the reddish-brown iron oxide-coated pebbles that covered the Nazca desert's surface, revealing the lighter-colored earth beneath. These shapes range in size from a few feet to more than 1,200 feet and depict animals, plants, geometric designs, and humans. The Nazca people created the lines by moving small stones from the ground and stacking them into shapes. They were created between 500 BCE and 500 CE for unknown reasons, and theories have abounded over the years regarding their purpose.

The Nazca Lines have been recognized as a World Heritage Site by UNESCO. They are an incredible testament to the creativity and skill of the Nazca culture, who used them as a form of devotion to the gods. They've served as inspiration for scientists, artists, and tourists from all over the world. Despite the many theories proposed, the true purpose remains a mystery.

Of note is that the Nazca Lines are so massive that they can only be seen entirely from the air. Curiously, the Nazca people had no access to any flying machines that would have allowed them to see what they were creating. Only in the twentieth century, when pilots started flying over the area, did the mystery of the Nazca Lines become more well-known. The wonder surrounding the Nazca Lines seems almost as mysterious as how they were created. Nevertheless, they remain an amazing example of ancient creativity and engineering that continues to inspire new theories about their origin and significance.

The Greenbrier Ghost

In the late 1800s, a strange and eerie event took place in a small town in West Virginia. It involved the death of a woman named Elva Zona Heaster, whose alleged return from the dead to testify against her husband in court made headlines across the nation.

Elva was known as the youngest daughter in a quiet and reserved family. However, in January 1897, her lifeless body was found in her home, with her husband Erasmus claiming she had died of natural causes.

But then, Elva's mother began to have strange and vivid dreams in which her daughter appeared and told her that she had been murdered by her own husband. Persuaded, authorities exhumed Elva's body for examination, and to their shock, she had a broken neck.

Shue's trial was a scene straight out of a horror movie. Elva's ghostly apparition made an appearance and spoke loudly, testifying that Shue had killed her. The jury was so moved by this otherworldly testimony that they found Shue guilty of murder, sentencing him to life in prison.

The story of the Greenbrier Ghost case quickly gained national attention. It sparked both fascination and fear among people, with many intrigued by the idea that a ghost helped solve a crime. It also highlighted the dark reality of domestic violence and how women had been mistreated by their husbands during this time period.

The tale of the Greenbrier Ghost inspired books, plays, and even a ballet. It's the only instance in history in which a ghost has been used as evidence in a court of law. Today, it remains a peculiar and captivating footnote in American history, a popular topic in discussions about the justice system and women's rights.

The Highgate Vampire Panic

Highgate Cemetery was once a quiet, overgrown resting place for the wealthy of London. However, in the late 1960s and early 1970s, it became the site of a supernatural panic that enticed both locals and paranormal enthusiasts alike. Reports of a mysterious entity with glowing eyes and sharp teeth roaming the cemetery soon spread. Some believed it to be a vampire, while others claimed it was a revenant or a demonic spirit.

Amid the growing hysteria, thrill-seekers visited the cemetery, hoping to catch a glimpse of the supernatural being. Some even performed rituals and conducted séances to communicate with the entity. The frenzy reached its peak with large crowds gathering outside the cemetery walls at night.

The event's most prominent figure was Sean Manchester, a self-proclaimed bishop and exorcist who claimed to have encountered the infamous entity. Manchester's claims led to widespread concern and fear of the danger that the Highgate Vampire posed to the community. The media covered the panic in detail, causing a surge of interest in the paranormal and fear of the unknown.

However, despite the legend of the Highgate Vampire remaining popular to this day, the event has been debunked as either a hoax or a misidentification of more mundane phenomena. The panic raised concerns about the safety and security of the cemetery, resulting in increased security measures and fencing around the graveyard.

The Highgate Vampire Panic is now recognized as an example of the power of the media and popular culture and their ability to create and maintain urban myths and legends. It is seen as a cautionary tale of the dangers of irrational beliefs and mass hysteria. While the Highgate Vampire remains a popular topic in paranormal circles, most people consider it a product of the collective imagination rather than a real threat.

The Cleveland Clinic Fire of 1929

Back in 1929, the Cleveland Clinic was renowned worldwide for its high-level medical research and groundbreaking treatments. But on May 15th of that same year, the hospital would make headlines for a far less desirable reason. An unfortunate fire broke out in the building, resulting in a devastating loss of life and the destruction of the hospital.

Despite Cleveland's bustling scene and advancements in medical practices, fires were a common threat in most buildings during that time. The Clinic was not immune to such risks. Although the exact cause of the fire is unknown, it's believed to have started due to an electrical short circuit in the research building's basement.

From there, the fire spread rapidly, engulfing the whole facility in a matter of minutes. The fire department and Cleveland Clinic staff mobilized quickly to evacuate patients and contain the disaster, but a lack of safety equipment and modern building materials made their efforts futile.

The fire had catastrophic consequences, claiming the lives of 123 people, including doctors, nurses, and patients. But out of the ashes of tragedy came a new era of fire safety. In the wake of the Cleveland Clinic Fire of 1929, new regulations and standards were implemented across the United States. Non-combustible materials, fireproofing, and flame-resistant equipment became mandatory for public buildings, making them safer for all.

Regardless of the heartbreak and devastation that the community faced, Cleveland's medical efforts were resilient and bounced back stronger than ever. The clinic was able to rebuild within a year with advanced fire suppression and detection systems. From then on, the Cleveland Clinic was one of the safest hospitals in the world, providing exceptional care to patients while prioritizing fire safety.

Today, the Cleveland Clinic Fire of 1929 serves as a stark reminder of why fire safety is critical in public buildings. The catastrophic disaster led to significant changes that still influence building codes and regulations today. And though the tragedy took place almost 100 years ago, it continues to fascinate and inspire as a reminder of what can happen when safety measures are ignored.

The Great Garlic Mystery in France

One summer in 2019, French garlic crops began to disappear from fields all over the country. This strange occurrence soon became national news, leaving farmers, scientists, and the government scrambling for answers. Garlic is significant to French cuisine and agriculture, with Provence being well-known for producing some of the world's best. Unfortunately, in recent times, the farming industry has been under pressure due to climate change and trade policies, posing new threats to their livelihoods.

As the thefts became more frequent, farmers began reporting the disappearance of their crops to the authorities, but with no explanation. The thieves appeared to be professionals, targeting the finest varieties and leaving no trace behind. Investigators quickly began to investigate, but they came up empty-handed.

Scientists conducted tests to investigate the possibility of disease or pest infestation, but all results came back negative. Additionally, the geographic distribution of the thefts puzzled investigators as the garlic disappeared randomly and not in any particular region.

The Garlic Mystery had a severe impact on farmers' livelihoods as the prices for the remaining bulbs skyrocketed, driving many small producers out of business. The agricultural sector as a whole suffered massive losses from this event. The government pledged to improve security for farmers, but this has yet to happen. As a result, it sparked discussions about supporting local agriculture, ensuring its security, and preserving food security in France.

The Garlic Mystery created a media frenzy and sparked a flurry of garlic-related conspiracy theories. Some claimed that foreign governments were to blame, while others pointed fingers at rival garlic producers. Garlic thefts are not unusual in France, but the scale and mystery surrounding this event captured the public's attention.

In contemporary times, the Garlic Mystery serves as a cautionary tale for French farmers and a source of fascination for garlic enthusiasts. This event highlighted the precarious state of the country's agricultural industry, leading to discussions on how to support small producers, protect against agricultural crime, and maintain food security.

The WOW! Signal

The world of astronomy has been captivated by one unexplainable signal: the WOW! Signal. Jerry Ehman, an astronomer at Ohio State University, made a groundbreaking discovery in 1977 - a mysterious radio signal picked up by the Big Ear radio telescope during his data analysis. This cataclysmic event is not only a significant scientific feat but also an exciting topic for the book "100 Unbelievable Events That Actually Happened".

The search for extraterrestrial intelligence is nothing new, but the invention of radio telescopes added a new dimension to their quest. With the Big Ear telescope, scientists worked to identify radio signals that could potentially come from intelligent extraterrestrial life.

The signal spotted by Jerry Ehman was no ordinary transmission. It lasted for 72 seconds and was 30 times stronger than usual laboratory background noise. So unprecedented was the signal that Ehman circled it on the printout and wrote "WOW!" next to it. The signal disappeared completely after, despite numerous attempts to locate another instance.

To this day, the WOW! Signal remains one of the most debated unsolved queries in the world of astronomy. The signal's origin baffles experts and has sparked various discussions as to the plausibility of extraterrestrial life. However, this particular event had other ramifications as well. The renewed attention to the search for extraterrestrial intelligence led to increased funding, reinforcing efforts to probe the universe further in search of answers.

The signal came from the direction of the Sagittarius constellation, leading some to speculate that it could have come from a planet orbiting one of the stars in that region. Another fascinating fact is that Jerry Ehman failed to recreate the signal using his toaster. Moreover, according to experts, the frequency of the signal customarily blocked by the Earth's atmosphere is what makes the WOW! Signal extraordinary.

Today, the WOW! Signal remains a topic of public fascination, continually being referenced in popular culture in movies and TV shows. While a conclusive answer to the signal's origin still eludes us, the possibility of finding another that could potentially unravel the mysteries of the universe keeps the search going.